𝒫𝒽... 𝒞. 𝒪.

"Before I ever opened ▮▮▮▮▮ ᴉe, prompting me to want ▮▮▮▮▮ ᴉd began to read, Carey's ▮▮▮▮▮ ᴼn about who we are or w   MW01059491   ty of who we are is walkiᴨ... ᴨ.. ... ᵇʸ ᵒᵃʸᴵᴵᵍ ᵧᵒᵘ ᴵᵒ ᴵᴵᵃᴵᴵᵉᴵ ᵛᵛᴵᴵᵃᴵ. ᵓᵘᴵᴵᴷᴵʸ, I noted the following quote in my journal, *Being uncommon in this world takes a strong woman with some guts and grit.'* I am fired up and ready to step back in and be *Uncommon.* Thank you, Carey!"
—Shari Rigby, Actress, *October Baby*, Director of
The Dream Center, Speaker, and Writer of *Beautifully Flawed:*
Finding Your Radiance in the Imperfections of Your Life

"If you're comfortable with mediocrity, don't bother opening this book. But if you've been longing to escape the mundane? . . . Throughout these pages, you'll hear the voice of the best kind of friend: one who's been there, who gets where you're at, and who wants to see you grow far beyond the status quo. Carey equips you to step boldly into the intentional, countercultural, uncommon life God created you for and calls you to live."
—Cheri Gregory, Coauthor of *Overwhelmed:*
How to Quiet the Chaos and Restore Your Sanity

"Being uncommon in this world takes a strong woman with some guts and grit. I give a big yes and amen to that. Carey has written this book so beautifully, while filling it with such practical life-changing insights and encouragement. You will be encouraged to live an uncommon life, no matter what comes your way."
—Alli Worthington, Author of *Breaking Busy: How to Find Peace and*
Purpose in a World of Crazy and *Fierce Faith: A Woman's Guide*
to Fighting Fear, Wrestling Worry and Overcoming Anxiety

"In a world that seems to be in a race to the lowest common denominator, Scott calls us higher with *Uncommon.* She surrounds us with a crowd of exemplary women from scripture, equips us with verses to cling to and prayers to pray, and pushes us forward with the voice of a friend and coach. *Uncommon* is the book that's needed for women of our day."
—Amy Carroll, Author of *Breaking Up with Perfect*,
Proverbs 31 Ministries Speaker and Writer

"Carey Scott takes the word 'uncommon' and unpacks it into a positive experience through the lens of Scripture. This book is saturated with depth—something women are seeking as they dig into their own identities as daughters of the King. You'll want to read it twice: once alone as you cry, and again with a group of friends on the same journey of uncommon womanhood. Get out your highlighters and get started on this book today!"
—Christine Abraham, Founder and
Ministry Director at Women's Bible Café

"*Uncommon* offers honesty, vulnerability, and courage that will challenge you in a world that is screaming, 'Not enough!' Carey is lovable and beyond inspiring as she shares her vulnerabilities and personal stories that will make you laugh out loud and cry at the same time. A heartfelt and tender read that will move you, captivate you, and encourage you to be. . .uncommon."

—Melody Lovvorn, Co-Founder of Undone Redone,
Creator of My Secure Family & Perfectly Imperfect Marriage

"Every fiber of our being craves comfort. Add that to the pull of our fears, our selfishness, our desire to not make waves, and we can easily live a 'safe,' but unremarkable life. Carey issues a loving, beautiful challenge to live life boldly, deliberately, to dare to be different in a world that demands conformity. She writes with such beautiful authenticity because, well, she's not normal. And I mean that in the best possible way. Carey is living the uncommon life. Over and over again, she uses real-life and biblical examples that powerfully illustrate the amazing and sweet God who meets us when we dare to live a life that, choice-by-choice, reflects His uncommon love, boldness, kindness, and generosity. A life that is anything but normal, but one that leaves us in grateful awe of the mind-blowing grace and power He is just waiting to display through us."

—Melinda Means, Speaker and Author of Invisible Wounds:
Hope While You're Hurting

"Carey's words pack a powerful punch from the very first page. This book gives us permission to step away from perfectionism and into the life of freedom God desires for us. If you're looking for peace, if you're ready to make a change in your life, if you want the freedom of heart promised by God, this is a guidebook to get you there. I cried, I laughed, I pondered. . .and most of all, I found myself reflected in Carey's words."

—Jill Hart, Founder of Christian Work at
Home Ministries and Author of Do Life Different

"A refreshing and motivational call-to-action, Carey Scott offers us another book filled with wisdom, insight, and down-to-earth girl talk—a how-to for adding depth and beauty to our daily lives."

—Varina Denman, Author of Looking Glass Lies

"As Christians, we are called to live differently, but how should we do this? Often we think it's about standing up for and upholding what we believe are Christian principles. Carey teaches us another way. She champions us to stand out from the crowd and be extraordinary in our ordinary day-to-day moments and encounters. However, Carey never asks us to do anything she hasn't done or wouldn't do herself. She draws us in through her struggles, many common to all of us, and encourages us to be Uncommon."

—Rachel Britton, Writer, Blogger, and Speaker

"Through what truly felt like comfortable conversation with a good friend, Carey reminded me why it matters deeply that believers live the way God intended—as salt and light. Every chapter encouraged me with examples of women in the Bible who modeled this kind of life and were blessed for it, along with very practical action steps that convinced me I really can do hard things! Uncommon is one of those rare and wonderful books I enjoyed from start to finish and will no doubt be pulling back off the shelf to refer to again and again for personal accountability and for guidance in mentoring others."

—Amy Hale, Online Bible Study Leader and Teacher

Un-Common

PURSUING A LIFE OF
PASSION AND PURPOSE

CAREY SCOTT

SHILOH RUN PRESS
An Imprint of Barbour Publishing, Inc.

Dedication

This book is dedicated to the woman who has believed
for so long that being different isn't a bad thing.
Maybe you've had it right all along.
Good for you.
Rock on, sister.

Acknowledgments

Wayne, you are a one-in-a-million kind of husband, and your unwavering support makes what I do possible. Thank you for carrying an extra load from time to time so I can walk out my calling. Thank you for being a cheerleader when I doubt my words. Thank you for being an encourager when I feel unworthy. Thank you for putting up with my crazy. Such a man is uncommon.

Sam and Sara. You two are why I want to be uncommon! I want to give you a compelling reason to live differently than the world. I want to teach you to love with all you have and know right from wrong with the same measure of passion. You are the next generation of influencers, and I am excited to watch as your lives point others to God. You are extraordinary, and I love being your mom.

Jessie Kirkland, the most amazing agent to walk planet earth, you may never know how much I treasure your friendship. You've fought for me and my work in uncommon ways, through the best times and the hardest times, and I'm sure your heavenly crown will be fitted with the biggest jewel on record. I promise to help you hold your head up from its weight. You are—hands down—one of my favorites.

To Lisa Kyle, Julie Thomas, Sherry Snead, and the rest of my powerful tribe of warriors, you have worked overtime to keep me sane. Litcrally. Thank you for being available. Thank you for being willing to walk into deep waters with me. And thank you for pouring your love and wisdom into my life. You are the very essence of uncommon.

Kelly McIntosh and the entire team at Barbour Publishing, thank you for saying yes to *Uncommon*. That you would want to publish a book like this tells me you're a different kind of house. I couldn't be more excited to partner with you.

And thanks to you—the sweet woman holding this book. I wrote these words *for* you and *because* of you. As I typed away at my computer, I kept seeing your face, and it spurred me on. My hope is that you develop passion for the truth as you learn to walk out your God-created purpose. What a gift you will be to the world as you do. Through these pages, God is calling you higher. He is calling you deeper. And I am challenging you, #beUncommon.

Contents

CHAPTER 1

The Common Life

$\mathcal{I}$ laid my hands on my belly and prayed right there in the kitchen.

Father, I don't want this. My family needs me. Please don't ask me to carry this burden. But Lord, if this is part of Your perfect plan—and if my journey will help one woman find You—I'll take it.

That day, in all my fear and anxiety and confusion, with tears spilling out of my eyes, after weeks of being in a fetal position, I accepted the possible assignment of ovarian cancer. The pathology report from a routine I-don't-want-my-period-anymore hysterectomy showed a small spot on my uterus with ovarian cancer cells. And four different pathologists found it.

Cancer.

It's the word we dread more than any other. It's the diagnosis we never want to hear. And my doctor spoke it as we sat in the exam room. I could tell something wasn't right when I first saw her face, but *this* had never crossed my mind. Cancer wasn't part of the plan. My appointment that day was to remove stitches. Not this. And as my two kids— then seven and eight—enjoyed extra screen time as they sat in the waiting room, their only concern was what flavor of ice cream they were going to order at Dairy Queen on the way home.

But my concern was heavy enough for all of us.

Am I going to die? That was my next question—one with no immediate answer. I'd have to meet with an oncologist who would run tests to get a better understanding of the spot and the cells, and then determine the next steps. But that wasn't now. Now was the time I had to muster every bit of strength so I could hold it together for my kids. Now was when I had to get control of my thought life so I didn't fall into the pit of hopelessness. Now was the season when I needed to press into God with all my might so I could navigate this situation well.

I gathered my kids and drove to Dairy Queen. It took determination not to burst into tears as I watched them eat their ice cream from the rearview mirror. I was so thankful for the oversized sunglasses. They were the only thing hiding the fear and confusion in my eyes. And when we got home, I turned on a movie to distract them as I slipped away into my bathroom to gather my thoughts. I called my husband and my parents and others who needed to know. And then I lost it.

The cancer center waiting room was decorated with great intentions of bringing light and hope to those who sat it in. But regardless, it was filled by patients and family members with empty, blank stares. And as I sat there with my husband, I silently prayed for God to intervene.

The oncologist was cold and young, and he ran lots of tests that involved needles—something that unnerved me even more. We listened as the doctor made the case for removing my ovaries and possibly more based on what they had discovered. At that point, neither of us would argue with his suggestions. I couldn't help but feel sorrowful that a part of what made me a woman was about to be removed.

This choice wasn't for me to make—it was a choice made for me. It's funny how you define yourself as a woman by the organs that help create or sustain life. Maybe you know just what I'm talking about.

And I began asking God tough questions: *Why do bad things keep happening to me? When is enough. . .enough?*

Let's just say I haven't lived a charmed life. From sexual abuse at age four to a minefield of other painful encounters with men growing up to an embarrassing divorce with my first husband plus a million more "you've got to be kidding me" moments, life had been anything but charming. Or easy. And because I thought maybe God would let the second half of my life ease up, I certainly didn't see this coming. I was at the crossroads of *questioning* God and *trusting* God, and I had a choice to make.

He brought back to mind a vision from years earlier where He revealed plans for a speaking ministry. And I had watched in awe as random invitations to speak came my way. God had been opening doors only He could open. So deep down, I knew He was trustworthy and had good plans for my future. But this was real life in Technicolor, and I wondered if I could trust God in this life-and-death situation, too.

The timing was horrible. My husband and I were in crisis mode with our son, who was reeling from the horrible and painful effects of a third-grade bullying situation. He needed me now more than ever. And my daughter needed a mom to teach her about being a woman of God, something I was excited and honored to share with her. I knew my husband didn't want to think about raising this family without me. We'd fought hard for the marriage we had, and the thought of being apart was too much. *I can't die now. My family needs me. Why is this happening?*

It's easy to trust God when the stakes are low, but this wasn't one of those times. There was so much to lose. . .so many lives to mess up. . .so many dreams hanging in the balance. Believe me, God and I had conversations. Lots of them. But with each prayer, with each scripture read, with each worship song that passed through my lips, things began to shift in me. Fear became hope. Anger became resolve. And questions became praise.

I decided to reach out on social media, asking for prayer and sharing my journey. I'm pretty sure I was on every prayer list from LA to NYC. My online community rallied around me in such a profound way—an uncommon way. And I felt loved and cared for and encouraged with each message and post. This unexpected support system blessed me more than I can even put into words. Community is a powerful weapon.

So as I stood in the kitchen that day praying and laying my own hands on the part of my abdomen directly in front of my ovaries—standing at the intersection of *questioning* and *trusting*, of *fear* and *courage*—an immediate calm overcame my heart, and worry gave way to bravery. And in an instant of complete surrender, I told my Creator that if it was His will for cancer to be part of my story, then so be it.

That response was anything but common. And it was a sharp left turn from what my prayer had been. Something had changed.

In that moment, God gave me a complete peace the world couldn't understand—a peace I couldn't even fully understand. His presence in the room was so thick, and I felt His supernatural strength infuse me. Even typing this out, I'm struggling to find the perfect words to describe an experience that was unexplainable. Maybe you know exactly what I am talking about because you've experienced it, too. There are powerful moments when God collides with our anxious hearts, and the results are profound. That sacred moment created a new resolve in me for the assignment I felt God might have ordained for me. And looking back— because I didn't realize it then—I was making a conscious decision to be uncommon by saying. . .*yes*.

That's what God does for us when we seek Him. That's what happens when we press into the Perfect One for help. That's what happens when we give God permission to use our story. He exchanges our ordinary for extraordinary. But it's a choice—every day and in every situation. Being uncommon takes guts and grit and a willingness to surrender.

Some of those days between the doctor's diagnosis and my kitchen prayer time were pretty messy. I cried and screamed at God for letting this happen. I hid under the covers, feeling hopeless. I pleaded with God, reminding Him of the two kids He gave me to steward—ones who deeply needed their mama. I told God that while my husband was an amazing father, he would not make the best mother. And I began isolating myself. I hate good-byes.

Don't you think all of those responses make sense? Because when life throws punches and knocks us to our knees, sometimes we struggle to find a way to get back up again. It takes time to catch our breath and find our footing. Even if we're connected to the heart of God, sucker punches hurt. We still get scared. And even more, they can make us second-guess God and His ability and willingness to help us.

Maybe you've responded to life's surprises in these sorts

of ways in the past. These responses are not only common, but they make us mortal. Hey, we're not perfect, right? I call them "fleshy" moments because we take our eyes off God and act out of human emotions. We cower before the scary-looking giant standing in front of us. We let the fear of our circumstances seep into our thoughts. We feel small and vulnerable. And it scares us.

I completely understand what it's like to doubt God's sovereignty, faithfulness, or trustworthiness when we get scary news from the doctor. And when our future feels uncertain, I know how normal it is to let fear get the best of us. We've all struggled to love the unlovable and forgive the unforgivable, especially when they've been the cause of our pain. And we all have a rebellious streak (or four) that often entices us to ignore truth and respond the way that feels good in the moment. It's "normal." But friend, we weren't called to be normal.

Let's unpack the tendency we have to respond in "common" ways even further. Think back to a time or two when you should have persevered but instead gave up on something or someone because it just took too much effort. Do you remember having the perfect opportunity to share your faith, but you let it pass because you were worried what others might think of you? And who hasn't felt like their prayers hit the ceiling, so they just gave up asking? Too often, we decide waiting for God to intervene isn't working—we worry He is going to be late—so we try to fix it ourselves instead. And in the hustle and bustle of life, I bet we've all put God at the very end (or close enough) on our to-do list. Common, right?

Maybe you have a friend who is a cup-half-empty woman, so you avoid her calls rather than encouraging her to see life differently. Maybe they don't include you in the group, so you gossip behind their backs to help justify those feelings of rejection. Maybe your husband asks for forgiveness, but you're slow to give it because you enjoy the power. Or maybe you have the chance to give someone grace, but instead you allow your sense of justice to take over. Typical responses, yes?

Maybe your kids act out at school and you overpunish because you're worried their actions will make you look like a bad mom. Or when another kid is mean to your child at school, you heap blame on his or her mom and decide your own parenting skills are superior. When people cut you off on the freeway, you scream at them because they were wrong. And when life gets hard, you step into the victim role and milk the attention for all it's worth. Aren't those normal and justified?

The truth is that it's easy to yell in anger and gossip in our hurt. It's easy to give the silent treatment when someone makes us mad. It's easy to quit when it gets hard. It's easy to have a crisis of faith when God doesn't answer prayers the way we want them answered. It's easy to make quick decisions without seeking His will. It's easy to dislike others, especially when they stand for something different. And sister, this list isn't even exhaustive.

I'm guessing you found yourself somewhere in those last few paragraphs. Sweet mother, I know I did. Having these common responses to life is something that unites us, because we all have them—every single one of us. I'm not saying it's a good thing. I'm just saying it's a *normal* thing. Can you see how easy it is to live the common life? It has become our default button, and here's why. . .

Most of us were taught to go with the flow. . .follow the

crowd. . .fit in at all costs. . .avoid the spotlight. We were told to be normal—whatever that meant. We were taught to blend in so we would avoid standing out. We probably watched our parents try to live this way and took our cue from them. And so we grew up doing the same thing everyone else was doing, because we learned the hard way that being different—being uncommon—was unacceptable.

Most of us weren't encouraged to be special or to stand out. And if we were, it was only to an acceptable or appropriate level. Few of us felt comfortable rocking the boat too much because we might get noticed for the wrong things. We weren't encouraged to take risks and try new, inventive ways of doing things. Instead, we learned to follow the leader and stick to the unwritten rules within our families and even in our culture. We didn't want to do anything that might bring criticism, judgment, or negative labels our way, so we opted for the status quo. And if we did choose to be different or step out in another direction, it was probably because everyone else was doing it, too. No wonder we are where we are today.

If you journeyed through my last book *Untangled: Let God Loosen the Knots of Insecurity in Your Life*, my hope is God uncovered places where you didn't (or don't) feel special. I pray He revealed and healed *I'm-not-good-enough* lies that knotted up your confidence as a woman, a wife, a mom, a friend, and a daughter. These lies have the power to make us feel ordinary because they trigger feelings of inferiority and insignificance, so we fly under the radar, hoping to be unnoticed. And through the pages of *Untangled*, we learned prayer and scripture are fail-safes to keep us from falling into the pit of common living. Even if you didn't read *Untangled*, God's willingness to free you is just as real.

When we invite Him into our broken places, we experience freedom. The chains that have held us hostage fall away. They are lying at our feet. And when we choose to walk away from them in our God-given freedom—freedom to believe we're good, lovable, and worthy, freedom from worrying if we have what it takes to be the woman God created us to be, freedom from being consumed by what others think of us, freedom from trying to fit into the world's ways—we can live uncommon. God is the key.

Take a moment right now and close your eyes. Can you bring a visual of that beautiful image to mind? Now spread your arms wide, take a deep breath, and feel the freedom. See yourself taking a step away from what has tangled you for so long. The chains can't hold you anymore. Can you see it? You are no longer a prisoner to common ways of living. Your insecurities can't keep you afraid of standing out. Friend, it's uncommon and it's the way God created you to live.

Freedom is so powerful. And sometimes when it's new, it feels foreign. Unfamiliar. You wonder, *What now?* And it's in that unfamiliarity that we often reach down, pick up those entanglers, and try to wear them again. They have been your identity for so long. For many of us, they're all we've known, and we fear changing what's always been. We begin to crave the common life because we know how to navigate it.

When Moses led the Israelites out of their four hundred years of slavery in Egypt and into the desert, these men, women, and children tasted glorious freedom—freedom they had been crying out to God for daily. In the wilderness, gone were the days of abuse and oppression and they instead traveled with visual reminders that God was with them. But less than three months after their miraculous exodus, they wanted Egypt again. It was familiar and predictable. And they romanticized their bondage, forgetting the hopeless conditions that smothered them.

"It would have been better if we had died by the hand of the Eternal in Egypt. At least we had plenty to eat and drink, for our pots were stuffed with meat and we had as much bread as we wanted. But now you have brought the entire community out to the desert to starve us to death" (Exodus 16:3 VOICE). Every time I begin to feel disgusted by their lapse in judgment, I'm reminded of my own. I understand their argument for the familiar.

But friend, you cannot live extraordinary when you live in the bondage of ordinary. You weren't just created to survive. You were created to thrive.

Countless times, I've seen women opt for bondage rather than embrace the freedom God had delivered them into. I've actually been one of them—more than once. But how can we continue to justify that kind of living when we collide with Galatians 5:1? *"Christ has set us free to live a free life. So take your stand! Never again let anyone put a harness of slavery on you"* (MSG). We can't justify it at all because freedom and bondage cannot coexist. Neither can uncommon and common. We have to choose which life we want. So let's choose right now.

Remember the picture in your mind's eye of standing in freedom with the tangling chains and ropes now lying at your feet? Rather than choosing to be tied to an ordinary life again, why not accept freedom and walk into a different way of living?

Will it be easy? Probably not. But that's okay. You can do hard things.

Will it be quick? Not necessarily. You didn't get here overnight, and healing won't be spontaneous either.

But I can promise you this: it will be so good. Why? Because choosing God's way over the world's way will reestablish your God-given identity. And when that happens, you'll begin to walk in the truth that you were created on purpose for a purpose. Rather than live in your own strength, you'll draw from God's strength so you can live differently—live with passion and purpose. That is how you live uncommon.

This book is all about *that* next step. It purposes to answer the question: *What does it look like to be uncommon?* I believe God will show us the way as we pursue Him. He will honor our desire to live with purpose and passion. In these pages, we'll unpack practical ways we can be different because the world needs the influence of uncommon women now more than ever. And God is extending an invitation for you and me to live in such a way that others see Him because of it.

We can't afford to sit on the sidelines any longer. Let's stop letting the Enemy discourage us into complacency. We don't have time to sit around in our mess, playing victim and making excuses. The world needs Jesus now.

Yes, it will require you to make hard choices and decisions. And yes, you will have to go against the norm. But we can do it all if we ask God for help.

The truth is that you and I are here for a reason. We have been anointed for a beautiful purpose. And like it or not, our words and actions are meant to point others to God Himself. We are His plan A. There is no plan B. Choosing to live in common ways—ways that focus on fitting in where we were never designed to—will make us miss the point of our existence.

Let's do this together—me and you. I want my life to make a real difference in the corner of the world where God has placed me. The fact you're still holding this book in your hands is proof that maybe you do, too. I'm tired of being told I have to fit in, because I was created to stand out. Friend, so were you.

Now take a deep breath.

Find your resolve.

And buckle up.

Because it's time to be. . .*uncommon*.

CHAPTER 2

The Reason We Can Be Uncommon

*F*ive hours later, the surgery was over. My husband, my parents, and my dear friend sat waiting to hear something—anything. And as the doctor walked toward them, hope sprung up in their hearts.

"We cannot find any signs of ovarian cancer. We've cut and cut and cut. We ran pathology on biopsied parts during surgery, but they came back clean. And while we're sending some samples off to a lab for further testing, I feel confident we won't find anything."

Wait, what? Four different pathologists from four different labs found cells of concern that indicated cancer. Tests revealed lymph nodes of concern. And the surgeon found. . . *nothing*?

When he called a few weeks later confirming the post-op test results were indeed clean, he said no follow-up treatment was necessary. "So that's it?" And he replied, "That's it." I hung up the phone feeling gratitude, relief, and confusion—all at the same time.

Thank You, Lord.

I've often asked God how this fits into my testimony. Even today, I don't really understand what that season in my life was all about. Did He want my full surrender? Did sharing the diagnosis and asking for prayer within my community change someone's heart? Maybe I won't know the

.etails this side of heaven, but He wanted this story in the book. And maybe it's because I believe it was a miracle.

There are many people today who believe miracles don't exist. They believe in doctrine that says spiritual gifts—like healing—ceased with the original twelve apostles. They don't believe God performs signs and wonders anymore and think the New Testament miracles happened merely to prove a point. The term for this is *cessationism*, and I don't subscribe to it.

Now that doesn't mean I think every good outcome is a miracle, nor do I believe everything bad is courtesy of the Enemy. But friend, I've just seen God move too mightily in my life to have any other reasonable explanation for the disappearance of cancer. Maybe you have had the same experience. I look back at my life and see God's fingerprints all over it. And I'm humbled by all the ways He has worked in my circumstances—and in my heart. So I'm giving Him the glory and thanks for the favorable outcome. I firmly believe He answered prayer and healed my body.

The truth is we can't fully understand God. He is unpredictable. We don't know why He heals in some situations but not in others. We can't explain His actions, and so often His will and ways confuse us more than make sense. God just doesn't perform for us like some genie in a bottle. Our Father in heaven is the essence of uncommon, which by definition means He is exceptional and remarkable. And at some point, we have to embrace that truth and appreciate He cannot be boxed up or figured out.

Psalm 115:3 (MSG) reminds us that *"our God is in heaven doing whatever he wants to do."* He is sovereign. And even though I may not understand the details surrounding my diagnosis, the miraculous outcome, or why I had to face the harsh consequences of surgical menopause at a young age, I trust His reasoning. Romans 8:28 (VOICE) is why I can: *"We are confident that God is able to orchestrate everything to work toward something good and beautiful when we love Him and accept His invitation to live according to His plan."*

Chances are you've been confused by God in your life, too. And while He is never predictable, He is always trustworthy. God embodies everything uncommon. There is nothing normal about Him. Think about it. He doesn't react to circumstances like we do. He is quick to give grace, always acts justly, lives in peace, and has no sin. God's wisdom and understanding lack nothing. His ways are good and beneficial for all involved. Here's the perfect example.

To make a way for a renewed relationship, God's Son put on human skin and stepped out of a perfect heaven into an imperfect world. He allowed Jesus to die in brutality to bridge the gap left by sin. The cross was an uncommon way to show His love. God's complete forgiveness in that moment was an uncommon response to our sin. And Jesus' resurrection three days later was an uncommon way to validate Himself to humanity.

Here is where I am going to blow your mind. Ready? You—with all your flaws, faults, and failings—have the ability to be uncommon, too. And Genesis 1:27 tells us why.

In that short yet powerful scripture, we are told that we're created in His image. The Hebrew root of the Latin phrase for *image of God* is *imago Dei*. It means shadow or likeness. Simply put, you are a reflection of God.

That means because God is uncommon, you and I are uncommon, too. It's undeniable. We may not have His power, majesty, and authority, but we do have uncommon DNA running through our veins. You don't have to earn it. You can't lose it. And with the Holy Spirit's guidance, you have everything it takes to be uncommon. And it's not only an honor but also a responsibility.

Please reread that last paragraph. I need you to fully understand the truth of who you are because it's foundational. You were born to be different—to stand out. We all were, but we all won't. You have to make the choice to live that way, not perfectly but purposefully.

Being an uncommon woman means. . .

1) You rely on God more than yourself.
2) You find hope in the hard places.
3) You stand up for what's right.
4) You hold on to joy no matter what.
5) You're not afraid to step out of your comfort zone.
6) You're willing to risk your reputation as you live differently.
7) You don't give up or give in.
8) You don't live tangled by your past.
9) You look past your circumstances.
10) You understand there is a calling on your life.

Uncommon living isn't a call to be perfect. Perfection is a lie, and it's nowhere close to God's heart for us. Instead, uncommon living means we choose to live with passion and purpose.

Right about now, some of you might be struggling to feel worthy of such a call. All the times you've messed up are coming to mind. You feel sure past mistakes have wiped the uncommon-ness right off you. And maybe you've been told how very unspecial you are by mean-spirited people. The thought that someone like *you* could be exceptional seems silly because you feel as common as common gets.

And just when we think our past choices or current season of sinning disqualifies us altogether, we intersect with this passage of scripture. It's a powerful reminder that even in our messy lives, we have the ability to *be* uncommon. If you would allow me a little wiggle room to make a point, I want to show you what I mean. As I was writing this section of the book, God highlighted the scripture below and re-framed it in my mind, which deeply encouraged my heart! I hope it does for you, too.

Every time we run across the word *blessed* in the scripture below, we're going to replace it with the word *uncommon*. Just so we have the same frame of reference, the dictionary defines *uncommon* as something not often seen or experienced. It's remarkable and exceptional and is always above the ordinary. Now, sweet friend, soak this in from Matthew 5:1–12:

> *When Jesus saw his ministry drawing huge crowds, he climbed a hillside. Those who were apprenticed to him, the committed, climbed with him. Arriving at a quiet place, he sat down and taught his climbing companions. This is what he said:*
>
> *"You're ~~blessed~~ uncommon when you're at the end of your rope. With less of you there is more of God and his rule.*
>
> *"You're ~~blessed~~ uncommon when you feel*

you've lost what is most dear to you. Only then can you be embraced by the One most dear to you.

"You're ~~blessed~~ uncommon when you're content with just who you are—no more, no less. That's the moment you find yourselves proud owners of everything that can't be bought.

"You're ~~blessed~~ uncommon when you've worked up a good appetite for God. He's food and drink in the best meal you'll ever eat.

"You're ~~blessed~~ uncommon when you care. At the moment of being 'care-full,' you find yourselves cared for.

"You're ~~blessed~~ uncommon when you get your inside world—your mind and heart— put right. Then you can see God in the outside world.

"You're ~~blessed~~ uncommon when you can show people how to cooperate instead of compete or fight. That's when you discover who you really are, and your place in God's family.

"You're ~~blessed~~ uncommon when your commitment to God provokes persecution. The persecution drives you even deeper into God's kingdom.

"Not only that—count yourselves ~~blessed~~ uncommon every time people put you down or throw you out or speak lies about you to discredit me. What it means is that the truth is too close for comfort and they are uncomfortable. You can be glad when that happens—give a cheer, even!—for though they don't like it, I do! And

all heaven applauds. And know that you are in good company. My prophets and witnesses have always gotten into this kind of trouble." (MSG)

If you need to put the book down and dance around for a minute or shout a huge *amen* to the heavens, go ahead. I can wait. Seriously though, Jesus is telling us that being uncommon means we do life differently. It's seeing life differently. It's responding to life differently. And it doesn't mean life has to be perfect, and neither do we. It just encourages the heck out of me.

Before we move on, let me back up and set the stage for that mic-dropping passage. The Messiah's popularity had been on the rise, and everyone craved a piece of Jesus. They wanted to see Him. They wanted to hear Him. He was a big deal, and the disciples knew they were keeping company with a real celebrity A-lister. They were part of the "it" crowd now.

Can't you just imagine the huge temptation they faced in considering themselves superior to the common folk? Gosh, wouldn't you? Having Jesus as a flesh-and-blood friend would have easily exalted them in the eyes of others, and so He decided to address the temptation now. . .before their egos got the best of them. The goal in sharing the Beatitudes with them was to align their hearts with His truth and set them up with realistic expectations for the cost of being with Him.

These men needed to understand that walking with Jesus would open them up to persecution. They'd be misunderstood for choosing to live differently than the cultural norms. And because they chose to follow Christ, it also meant they were choosing not to seek worldly recognition and reward. He wanted to drive this point deep into the marrow of their bones. But He didn't stop there.

Jesus was an amazing communicator who knew when and how to bring perspective into a situation that would be a catalyst to shifting attitudes and hearts. And so He finishes with a powerful assurance to His followers. Jesus guarantees that their choice to live in uncommon ways would be fully acknowledged—if not in this life, then in the next. In other words, it would mean something. Their choice had great value in His eyes.

These Beatitudes should be an encouragement for us, too. Jesus uses them to contrast the differences between having an eternal focus (*which is uncommon*) and having an earthly response (*which is very common*). He is making a strong case for navigating life through spiritual eyes and ears, and Jesus wants us to understand that our hard choices aren't for nothing. Living uncommon is not a waste of time because God sees it all.

Every faith-filled *yes* is credited to us. And because His hope is for you and me to live with purpose and passion, we're cheered on by a cloud of witnesses as we choose an uncommon way of living in the real world. Jesus' challenge and guarantee wasn't just for the disciples. It wasn't only good back in the day. It is for us, too—here and now.

No one would argue that the way God wants us to live gravely contradicts with the boundary-pushing climate of the world we live in today. We'd be hard-pressed to find much commonality between the two. That means that living in uncommon ways will absolutely go against the grain. It's not meant to be a discouragement or to present a mountain too tall to get over. But like Jesus did for His disciples, I need you to know it may not always be easy. But I can promise you it *will* always be worth it. And friend, you can do hard things.

With the state of the world right now, I can't think of anything we need more than women who have the guts and grit to let their lives reek of Jesus.

But let's be honest with one another. Sometimes we need more than a *rah-rah let's be different* cheer to make us change from the status quo. It may all sound good and great. . .but when life is pretty comfortable and familiar, why should we shake things up? Sometimes we like being snarky and cynical. Sometimes we enjoy holding on to offenses. And so often, it's easier to accept the ever-changing morals of society than stand up for what's right. We wonder if we have the ability to change anything anyway.

For me—and maybe for you, too—there has to be a rock-solid, hard-core, life-altering, kingdom-building reason before I'll change it all and live differently. Change is hard, and it's messy, and I like the security of the known and familiar. I need the *why*.

Then I read the next section of Matthew 5, and verses 13–16 hit me right between the eyes and offer me the compelling reasons I need in plain English. Buckle up.

> *"Let me tell you why you are here.* ***You're here to be salt-seasoning*** *that* ***brings out*** *the* ***God-flavors*** *of this earth. If you lose your saltiness, how will people taste godliness? You've lost your usefulness and will end up in the garbage. Here's another way to put it:* ***You're here to be light, bringing***

*out the **God-colors** in the world. God is not a secret to be kept. We're going public with this, as public as a city on a hill. If I make you light-bearers, you don't think I'm going to hide you under a bucket, do you? I'm putting you on a light stand. Now that I've put you there on a hilltop, on a light stand—**shine**! Keep open house; be generous with your lives. By opening up to others, you'll prompt people to open up with God, this generous Father in heaven."* (MSG, emphasis mine)

And there it is—*plain as day, fully explained, and deeply compelling*—the *why*!

You and I are on planet earth to be salt-seasoning and light-bearers. This passage tells us to be generous with our lives, investing in and encouraging those around us. God created us to stand out in the world! And when we make the choice to live our lives differently than the group-think of society, it will release the unique God-flavors and God-colors into the world.

But we can say no. Uncommon living isn't mandatory as a Christ follower. Instead, it's a choice. And next to salvation, the second-best gift the cross gave us was the power to make choices. We get to make them every day and in every situation. But it's important to understand what will happen if we choose not to live uncommon.

In verse 16, Jesus addressed that thought. It tells us that when we choose to be uncommon in our words and actions, it will prompt others to open up to God. That means your life has the power to point others to Him. So if we invert that truth, when we choose *not* to live differently. . .an opportunity to influence our corner of the world with the Good News is missed.

If we want to make a difference for the kingdom, we have to decide to be an uncommon woman. We don't have to be perfect, but we must be purposeful so we flavor and light the world. And when we do, it will point others to the goodness of God. That is why you and I are on planet earth. Read this paragraph again. Let it sink in for a moment.

Here's truth. This way of life may be risky to your reputation. You might be called a prude or a goodie-two-shoes or even a Bible-thumper. It's not always the most popular path to take because it calls us to walk above reproach. And breaking from the norm can bring criticism and judgment our direction. It can strain relationships, especially when you're in one that's not glorifying to God. But here this loud and clear: it's so worth it.

We're invited to be a part of something bigger—something God planned in advance for us to do. You're alive on the kingdom calendar now for a reason. There's something in you that God needs the world to have now. And sweet one, He is asking you to help bring heaven to earth.

Being uncommon in *this* world takes a strong woman with some guts and grit. And yes, you have what it takes because God has outfitted you. He doesn't call the equipped. He equips the called. And you are called.

For too long, we've been living just like everyone else. Common people act the same, don't they? We've strived for the wrong things. Our moral compasses haven't been trained on God. We haven't stood up for what's right. We've wanted to blend in. . .fly under the radar. . .and avoid the negative spotlight. We've been trapped by our insecurities, afraid to stand out or stand up. And I'm tired of it. Something tells me you are, too.

In these next chapters, we're going to unpack the different ways we can live uncommon. Let's find out how to live with purpose and passion so we can impact the world for good. It will be a choice—every day and in every situation. And saying yes will set us apart and call us out of the ordinary.

To illustrate, I'm going to introduce you to women in the Word who were known for living in uncommon ways or making choices that went against the grain. Scripture is rich with women who faced societal stereotypes, family dysfunctions, fear, and rejection and chose uncommon responses anyway.

So often, we think those named in the Bible have "saint" status—like they were extra special. But they weren't. They are just like you and me. Personal situations and cultural circumstances may have been different, but they faced all the same insecurities we do today. They faced hard choices, too. Don't miss that. I want you to see how very real they were. Because doing so will deeply encourage your heart, remind you you're not alone, and give you motivation to take a stand in your own place in history.

So rise up, friend. Whether you are wealthy or poor. . . with children or without. . .married, single, or widowed. . . connected or an outcast. . .prominent or obscure. . .a home-maker or businesswomen. . .disenfranchised or determined. . . a leader or follower. . .you have uncommon DNA running through your veins. Let this be your battle cry. You are not weak. It's not too late. And nothing from your past disqual-ifies you.

Together, we can take a stand for what is right.

We can influence our corner of the world to live better.

We can make choices that point others to our Father in heaven.

And God will give us everything we need to live. . . uncommon.

CHAPTER 3

Uncommon Courage

*When I needed the Lord, I looked for Him; I called out
to Him, and He heard me and responded. He came and
rescued me from everything that made me so afraid.*
Psalm 34:4 VOICE

$\mathcal{T}$he thumping noise coming through the speaker system
was terribly distracting. And as I sat on the front row waiting for the event hostess to introduce me, I wondered how
I was going to speak over the noise. This wasn't going to be
pretty. Or easy.

Being new to ministry, this was only the second time
I had stood in front of an audience to share God's Word. I
may have looked the part on the outside, but on the inside
my insecurities were waging war on my confidence. And as
she began to read my intro, the rhythmic thumping sound
became louder. I began to silently pray in desperation, "Father, please help me. I can't do this!"

As the audience began to clap and I reluctantly stood
up to make my way to the stage, I felt the Holy Spirit say,
"Move the lapel mic from your left side to your right." And
in that moment before I turned to face the room full of
women, I realized the thumping noise was the microphone
picking up the pounding of my anxious heart! My fears had
been exposed, and everyone in the room had audible proof
that I was a nervous wreck. Awesome.

These thoughts were running through my mind, making

my heart race to keep up!

> *Does my less-than-lovely past disqualify me from ministry?*
> *What if I don't look professional or put-together enough?*
> *What if I have the wrong theology or misinterpret scripture?*
> *If I share too much about my struggles, will they judge me?*
> *Do I have what it takes to bring value to the event,*
>   *or will I be a waste of their time and money?*

Fear is a big deal. It doesn't just manifest in those we consider weak and lacking in faith. It is something even the bravest of us struggle with. And it has the power to not only tangle us in knots and inform every decision we make but be something we unknowingly pass right on down to our kids and even transfer to others we do life with. Fear is a virus that spreads, and so often it's what keeps us from choosing the uncommon way.

We read stories of courageous acts in the face of danger and are inspired by their bravery. It's the plot for any good book or action movie, and we're drawn to the grit of the victor. We know women who have battled through cancer and never given up hope. Or families who've suddenly lost a loved one and chose joy over despair. I've watched my son fight his way back from the devastating effects of bullying when giving in would have been easier. My daughter has worked through debilitating fears that often caused nightmares. We've all seen uncommon courage unfold in front of our eyes. We know what it *looks like* to be brave. But for many of us, it's not something we're able to muster for ourselves.

Please don't give up. Don't give in to fear and live in hopelessness. The part of the world God has called you to influence needs to see faith in action. . .because it's contagious. I know life is big. And yes, it's hard. But you can do hard things. And where your courage ends, God's is there to strengthen you through His endless courage.

Sometimes we are afraid of not being liked. We're afraid to say yes to an opportunity because we don't feel worthy of it or are afraid we'll let someone down. We're anxious about standing up for ourselves and sharing what we really think or feel, worried criticism might wound our already damaged self-esteem. Or rather than make the tough moral choices— the ones we feel passionate about—we go with the flow to avoid standing out or being embarrassed. Haven't we all allowed the fear of others to paralyze us?

We can't live uncommon lives if we're so consumed by what others might think of us. Being popular and well-liked isn't the goal for our time on earth. Be kind and love well, but for heaven's sake, don't be scared of being *you*.

Fear stirred up by the state of our world causes panic, too. It feels scarier now than when we were kids, doesn't it? Every time we watch the news there are stories of mass shootings, horrific terrorism, racial tension, political rants, new diseases, child abuse, natural disasters, sinister acts, etc. It makes me want to put a huge bubble over my family so we don't get exposed to it all.

Sometimes I don't want to be brave as much as I want to hide away. When I suggest the option of home-colleging my kids—something I'm only sort of joking about—my teenagers shake their heads and walk away. They don't want to major in the big hair bands of the '80s. Honestly though, I often want to hole up at home and shut out the world because it just feels safer. I think we'd agree that our goal isn't always to be brave—it's to have our family out of harm's way.

But God continues whispering into my heart that the world isn't falling *apart*. . .it's falling into *place*. There are events on the kingdom calendar that have the ability to scare us. And as the return of Jesus gets closer, the Word is clear that it's going to get darker. But even then, God promises to never turn His back on us (Deuteronomy 31:6). The fear may be real, but God is always available to help (Psalm 46:1). So let's keep an uncommon perspective with regard to the world's insanity. And for Pete's sake, let's stop letting the news be our Bible.

Fear can also rise up in us as we watch our faith come under attack more and more in our own country. While we can't relate to the persecution our brothers and sisters around the world experience, being a Jesus follower has become more and more unpopular. Hobby Lobby and Chick-fil-A have shown uncommon courage as corporations, standing up for their religious freedom at all costs. In the sports arena, we see the uncommon resolve of Tim Tebow and Russell Wilson, who stand firm in their faith even when belittled for it.

But for so many of us, we're choosing to tuck our faith away until we get home. If there was any time to shine your light into the world, it's now. Not in a judgmental, *I'm-better-than-you* way. That's not cool. But friend, we aren't doing society any favors by hiding Jesus. And even more, we were created to bring salt-seasoning and God-colors into the world.

So please don't stop praying in restaurants. Don't stop inviting your neighbors to church. Be courageous enough to live your faith out loud. Be bold and confident in what you believe. And no matter what the world might tell you, being a Christ follower isn't something to be ashamed of.

Now I'm about to drop a hard truth into your lap. Oh, I pray this sinks in deep because it's vital to cultivating the uncommon courage we desperately need. Ready? Here it is: agonizing over the opinions of others, fretting over the state of the world, and hiding your faith will keep you trapped in the common life.

How? Rather than be confident in your ability to think and act, you will instead cower under fear and pressure. Unless you lean into God more than into your fears, uncommon living won't even be available. You won't have the confidence to choose it. But having uncommon courage is a game changer. And Psalm 56:3–4 (AMP) confirms it. It reads, *"When I am afraid, I will put my trust and faith in You. In God, whose word I praise; in God I have put my trust; I shall not fear. What can mere man do to me?"*

When I am afraid, I will trust God. Yes, that is good truth right there. You see, friend, fear is in the opposite direction of God. You either decide to trust God or you decide to trust fear. It's *your* choice, and each has a completely different road map to living. One is the easy way and the other the hard way. One is driven by the world, and the other has an eternal perspective. One is the common way to respond, and the other is uncommon. One will feed your fear until it becomes overwhelming. The other will require guts and grit to choose differently but will leave you with a sense of accomplishment and God's approval. You get to decide.

Many of us have lived in fear for so long we may not even realize it's our default button. It manifests as anxiety, hesitation, uncertainty, paranoia, control and manipulation, self-preservation, worry, and nervousness. Fear distorts reality and warps our perspective on truth. It shuts us up, shuts us down, robs us of joy, makes us ineffective in the roles we play as women, and sidelines us in the game of life. But even more, it stops us from walking out our faith in a world that needs examples of godly women. If we're really serious about having uncommon courage, we need to recognize the role fear is playing in our lives and resolve to be brave instead. We need to ask God for courage—the courage He has in abundance for those who ask.

Of course, there is healthy fear. We pay our taxes because we don't want to be audited. We put on sunscreen to avoid sunburns. We teach our kids not to get in cars with strangers or touch a hot stovetop to keep them safe. And in countless places in the Bible, we're told to have fear of the Lord, which essentially means to have a healthy respect for Him. But when debilitating fear rules our lives, when it makes us second-guess our wise decisions, when it replaces our belief that God is ultimately in control and will come through. . .then fear is not healthy.

Esther

In the story of Esther—an orphan in a foreign land being raised by her uncle Mordecai until chosen as queen for King Xerxes—we see a powerful example of what it looks like to face huge fear and show uncommon courage. Esther's royal position wasn't an accident or luck, but rather a divine appointment that ultimately stopped the evil plan of Haman to exterminate Jews from the Persian Empire. Let me set the stage.

Mordecai was a Jewish official in the royal court who really ticked off Haman. Chapter 3:1–2 in the book of Esther tells us why: *"Soon afterwards King Ahasuerus appointed Haman (son of Hammedatha the Agagite) as prime minister. He was the most powerful official in the empire next to the king himself. Now **all the king's officials bowed** before him in deep reverence whenever he passed by, for so the king had commanded. But **Mordecai refused to bow**"* (TLB, emphasis mine). Uh-oh. Now he had done it.

Haman's pride was damaged, and he became furious. But Mordecai wasn't necessarily trying to anger him; it was a matter of religion. To bow would be the same as giving divine honor to a human creature.[1] And since he was a devout Jew, nothing would convince him to do it. Based on his bold actions, I'm sure this wasn't the first time Mordecai had shown uncommon courage.

Haman's anger quickly turned into the desire for an early holocaust. And when Mordecai overheard his plan, he went to Esther with the details and suggested she approach the king and intervene. This is where we find the often-quoted scripture from Esther 4:14 (VOICE) that reads, *"And who knows? Perhaps you have been made queen for such a time as this."*

I imagine Mordecai's life taught young Esther exactly what it looked like to do hard things. Maybe it was her uncle's resolve that gave her the nerve to make the next move, even knowing it might result in her potential death.

While the idea of approaching your husband may not be life-threatening (unless perhaps during football season), in that empire people weren't allowed to approach the king unless he sent for them—and this included Esther. Even being the queen of Persia, she still had every good reason to fear for her life. But she knew unless King Xerxes became aware of Haman's plan, her people were going to be murdered.

In chapters 5–7 of Esther, you can read how she used patience and wisdom to find the perfect way and the right time to inform the king. But I want to highlight the verse that encapsulates the uncommon courage of our heroine. It shows her resolve to move forward and be strong even though it could cost her life. She chose to step off the easy path and onto the one that requires so much faith to walk out.

*"Go and get all the Jews in Susa together; hold a fast and pray for me. Don't eat or drink anything for three days and nights. My servant women and I will be doing the same. After that, I will go to the king, even though it is **against the law**. If I **must** die for doing it, **I will die**"* (Esther 4:16 GNT, emphasis mine).

Sweet mother. This is a woman with some serious uncommon courage, and she knew how to use it. Esther called for reinforcements, prepared her heart, and went against protocol, risking everything for what she knew was right. She accepted the hard assignment. Now the courage you need may not put your life in danger, but don't discredit what it does require of you.

Wielding uncommon courage can be very messy because the people around you may not understand what you're doing. It may go against group-think and you'll be opening yourself up to criticism. And sometimes it's those kinds of things that keep us from being fearless. Other times, it's those things that make courage prevail.

Jael

Meet Jael. Strong and decisive, she was the wife of Heber the Kenite clan's leader. While they weren't part of the Israelites, they were on friendly terms with one another.

Now buckle up because you may be surprised by her bold actions. This woman was fierce. But rest assured, she was walking out God's will. She had the uncommon courage to finish what a man refused to do.

After the Israelites defeated them at the Kishon River, the Canaanite commander Sisera fled the scene and came to the camp of Heber, looking for safety. Jael quickly recognized him and offered to let him rest in her tent. She gave him a drink and a place to lie down, and before he fell into an exhausted slumber, he told her to keep his location secret. He trusted her. But when he was fast asleep, she drove a tent peg through his skull, killing him instantly. What a contrast from one of the most highly regarded virtues of the day, which was being a hospitable hostess.

You may wonder why I'm not only including a murderer in the pages of this book, but also recognizing her for uncommon courage. First of all—and let me be very clear—I am absolutely *not* condoning the act of murdering another human being. It goes against the laws of the land, and it's the sixth God-given commandment, which says, "*Thou shalt not kill.*"

While I believe the Word of God is complete truth, I also find it confusing at times. I know there are some things this side of heaven I won't understand. I also know that while Jael's actions are hard to reconcile, she was *absolutely* doing God's will. Scripture clearly backs it up. I may not understand the ins and outs of God's system of justice, but I know she did what He wanted her to do.

The reality is that she was part of a brutal culture. And because Barak—a skilled warrior and competent general—was reluctant to follow God's command, the prophetess

Deborah told him in Judges 4:9 (TLB), *"The honor of conquering Sisera will go to a woman instead of to you!"* And so it was. God raised up a woman to do the job. And it's her name that's honored and celebrated because she chose to do the hard thing. In Judges 5:24–27, Deborah praises Jael for demonstrating uncommon courage.

I can't imagine she spent nights dreaming about killing Sisera or woke each morning with the desire in her heart. My guess is that when the moment presented itself, she obeyed the stirring in her spirit and acted. And sometimes that's exactly the kind of courage we need—the courage to jump into action when the opportunity presents itself, even if doing the right thing includes a risk.

Jehobsheba

Jehobsheba also stands out for her courage. She was the only princess of the royal house, wife of a high priest, and sister to King Ahaziah of Judah. When the king was killed, their stepmother Athaliah was determined to take over the throne herself. Jehobsheba knew that meant Athaliah would kill all royal heirs (even her grandkids).

Motivated by compassion for her nephew Joash and a commitment to God, Jehobsheba and her husband smuggled the infant from the palace to the temple. She could save at least one of the heirs. He lived there until he was seven years old. Think of all the times she must have wondered if Athaliah knew she was up to something. Had she even noticed they were one short when the other royal heirs were murdered? This wasn't a quick act of courage like we saw from Jael. No, this was almost seven years of choosing uncommon courage each day.

At the end of that time, a coup was organized, Athaliah was executed, and Joash was placed on the throne. You can find this story in 2 Kings 11. Such a risky move set Jehobsheba up daily for a death sentence if caught, but she said yes anyway. And it's a good thing, because her uncommon courage preserved the royal line of Judah, which is where the Messiah would eventually come from. We are still receiving the benefits of her bravery today.

You have the opportunity to be courageous every day of your life. Many times, it will be small acts of courage that may go unnoticed by those around you. Other times it will be monumental, and your bravery will be played out in the public square for all to see. Some may be quick choices that seem like muscle memory, while others will be daring choices you'll intentionally make. But regardless, having the uncommon courage to overcome fears and live different than the status quo takes guts and grit. And God.

Psalm 34:4 (VOICE) reads, *"When I needed the Lord, I looked for Him; I called out to Him, and He heard me and responded. He came and rescued me from everything that made me so afraid."*

In other words, God *hears* us. . .He *responds* to us. . .He *rescues* us. And that means He gives us courage to face our fears so we can live in uncommon ways. And that is a promise He will make good on any time we need Him.

Remember the story I shared at the beginning of this chapter about the lapel mic picking up the pounding of my heart for the whole room to hear as I was about to speak? Well, despite my fear, I spoke that day. Sometimes we just have to put on our big-girl pants and do the *thang* even though we're scared half to death. It probably wasn't the best talk I've ever shared with an audience, but it was a victory because I didn't let my anxieties sideline me. God heard my prayers and gave me the nerve to do what He called me to do.

Maybe you're scared of failing or embarrassing yourself. You may feel completely inadequate. Maybe you've no idea where to start. Maybe the latest news story has you freaked out. Maybe there is something God wants you to do that seems insurmountable. There are a million reasons for us to be afraid. And while fear is a normal response to this life, you can't live there. You were created to have uncommon courage!

So speak up. Share your heart. Put yourself out there. Say yes even if your knees are knocking and your hands are shaking. Be present in the world. Remember God's strength is available to you. Don't give up. Don't give in. Always ask the Lord for help. And don't forget, you can do hard things. Now go do them.

Lean into Him

> "But no weapon will be able to hurt you; you will have an answer for all who accuse you. I will defend my servants and give them victory." (Isaiah 54:17 GNT)

> Go to the LORD for help, and worship him continually. (1 Chronicles 16:11 GNT)

> If you fall to pieces in a crisis, there wasn't much to you in the first place. (Proverbs 24:10 MSG)

He is ever present with me; at all times He goes
before me. I will not live in fear or abandon
my calling because He stands at my right hand.
(Psalm 16:8 voice)

I am always aware of the Lord's presence;
he is near, and nothing can shake me.
(Psalm 16:8 gnt)

He is not afraid of bad news. His heart remains
secure, full of confidence in the Lord.
(Psalm 112:7 gw)

Look into You

What role does fear play in your life?

What would your life look like if fear was no longer
an issue?

How would your situation change if you trusted
God more than your fears?

What scripture or biblical character from this chapter speaks to you the most?

Where is God asking you to have uncommon courage right now?

Live Uncommon

Lord, help me overcome my fears by giving me uncommon courage. I confess that fear has been unhealthy in my life, and I want to lean more into You than into the things that scare me. In Your Word, You promise to deliver me from them, and I am asking for You to make good on that promise today. I need Your confidence and strength so I can be bold and brave. I want to be fierce. And please help me live out the courage You give me! In Jesus' name, amen.

CHAPTER 4

Uncommon Evangelism

For I am not the least bit embarrassed about the gospel.
I won't shy away from it, because it is God's power to save
every person who believes: first the Jew, and then the non-Jew.
Romans 1:16 VOICE

*F*or God expressed His love for the world in this way: He
gave His only Son so that whoever believes in Him will not face
everlasting destruction, but will have everlasting life" (John
3:16 VOICE). This is hands down one of the most recogniz-
able passages of scripture. Fans hold signs with this address
at sporting events. People tattoo it on their bodies. It's on
bumper stickers, posters, bracelets, and the like. And while
everyone is busy telling us what the world needs now is love,
they're missing the truth that God has already filled the
heavens and the earth with love. . .completely and perfectly.
He did so by giving His only Son to us—even knowing the
brutal death Jesus would face at the hands of the ones He
came to save.

Now let me interject something right here. As a parent,
I cannot imagine sending my son (or my daughter, for that
matter) to be slaughtered for the common good. Making
them leave our home where there's love and compassion
and go into a foreign place of darkness and deceit is absolutely unfathomable. I may love you, but I would never, ever,
never sacrifice my child so that our relationship could be
mended. And when I allow my mind to wrap around God's

revolutionary act of love, I weep.

Friends, there has never been a demonstration of uncommon love more profound than this. You were so very significant and valuable to your Creator—even before you were a twinkle in your parents' eyes—that He couldn't stand the thought of not spending eternity with *you*. And because sin is unbearable to God, it separated us. Unless He took drastic measures, we'd be forever divided. So Jesus stepped off His throne and entered the world in a radical way and with a radical agenda. We may not understand what eternity without our Creator would be like, but God does. So sending Jesus into the world to become the ultimate sacrifice—paying the heavy price of every sin we have or will ever commit—repaired once and for all our broken relationship. And it was 100 percent motivated by love.

That was two thousand years ago. And while His love for us has never changed, the world has. It's darker, filled with perversions of all kinds. Activists work to erase the name of God from our currency, our schools, and our government buildings. Hate groups spout off anti-God rhetoric. But it's not just in the United States. Russia recently passed a law that prohibits evangelism anywhere outside a church or religious site—including private homes and online—and those in breach of it will be fined. In China, more than two thousand crosses have now been forcefully removed from churches as part of a government campaign to regulate "excessive religious sites."[2]

Yes, the world most certainly needs love. But even more, what the world needs now is. . .*us*. I'm not speaking out of turn when I suggest that the American church needs to stop hitting the SNOOZE button. It's time to wake up. We are alive at this time on the kingdom calendar for a reason. This is our moment to make a difference by doing the very thing we were sent here to do. . .share Jesus. And with the state of the world, we don't have the luxury of pressing the SNOOZE button any longer. This is our time to evangelize.

Evangelism by definition means to spread Christianity through your *activities*. It's trying to persuade someone to share your enthusiasm for specific beliefs and ideals. But evangelizing doesn't always look the same. Not by a mile.

Maybe you have walked by someone holding a sign that said something like IF YOU DON'T HAVE JESUS, YOU'RE GOING TO HELL! Or maybe you've seen people standing on corners with megaphones shouting judgment and condemnation, trying to scare people into believing. Or maybe you've been handed a flyer as you pass someone on the street that tells you all the reasons you won't spend eternity with God. These are common forms of evangelism, but they are not the kind I'm suggesting.

Remember the beginning of John 3:16 where it said that *"God expressed His love for the world in this way"*? And remember we talked about the love God showed for us through the unimaginable act of sending His Son to pay the price for our sins? Well, it started and ended with one key ingredient. . . *love*. Knowing that, I'd like to propose that for us to be uncommon evangelizers we need to keep three things in mind:

1) Love needs to be our motivation.
2) Condemnation or scare tactics aren't productive.
3) Truth needs to be laced with kindness.

I have a longtime friend who is deeply involved in Wicca,

a "religion" often associated with witchcraft, occultism, and neo-paganism. It's not the same as satanism, and most witches don't even believe in the existence of Satan. Instead they live by one central rule called The Rede, which says, *"Harm no one, do what you will."*

My friend is kind and fun. She brings joy into a room with her bubbly personality and treats others respectfully. She volunteers her time, celebrates life's milestones with fervor, and bends over backward to help someone who needs it. She is a *good* person, but from what I understand, she is not a *saved* person. There is a difference. Ephesians 2:8–9 reminds us that *faith* saves us, not *works*. So when she surprised me by opening the door to discuss Christianity, I cautiously yet enthusiastically walked right through it.

We met over a series of dinners. She explained why she felt Wicca was the right religion, and I shared why I stood by faith in Jesus. Interestingly, she grew up in the church but was deeply hurt by it—so much so that she completely walked away from it as a teenager. She felt strongly that Wicca was what she needed to find peace and comfort. I validated her pain, saying churches were filled with broken people trying to figure out life, but that Jesus came to save the broken and He was incapable of inflicting emotional pain.

Most of us have a story of being wounded by the church. And too often, the ending to the story is the decision to walk away from faith altogether. Gosh, it's hard when people develop their opinions of God based on His followers. While we try to do the best we can, so often we're horrible poster children for faith. Many of us are hurting people who hurt people. That's why we need a Savior. That's why Jesus came. That's what I was trying to share with my friend.

Our times together weren't stressful because we gave each other freedom to talk candidly about our differing beliefs. There wasn't any condemnation or judgment. We weren't trying to forcefully win each other over to the other side. We were just two girls sharing our hearts.

Then the question came—the one I was dreading the very most. "So you're saying that because I don't believe Jesus is the Son of God. . .I am going to a hell that I don't even believe exists?" Gulp. I sat there for what seemed like five minutes staring down at my iced tea. Sometimes evangelizing requires us to answer tough questions. It's not that I'm ashamed of the Gospel or confused about what the Word says on this subject; I just knew I had to present this heavy truth the right way.

So I took a deep breath, looked her in the eye, kept my voice calm, took her hand, and said quietly, "Well, yes. That's what the Bible says. They aren't my words; they're God's. And because I choose to believe that all scripture is God-breathed, the answer to your question is. . .yes." The next few minutes were filled with the usual questions and comments, but it was an honoring discussion.

As we got up to leave, she hugged me and said, "Thank you for being honest with me. And thank you for talking without throwing fire and brimstone in my direction. I'm not sure I buy into that stuff, but you're the first Christian that hasn't tried to be something she's not and look down on me for believing differently. I'm really glad I know you."

And just like that, the door of discussion closed. I may never know if the seed God planted through our conversations ever fully bloomed. We don't keep up much anymore. But in her opinion, the truth was shared with her in an uncommon way.

For that one conversation I handled right, there have been so many more I've not. Maybe even the idea of having these kinds of conversations makes you sweat. They can be tough. Not everyone has the gift of gab or the confidence to boldly lay it out there. But I want to remind you of something very important: *every day you wake up, you are evangelizing.* I once read that we may be the only Bible someone reads. So while you may not preach with your mouth, you are most certainly preaching with your life.

Think about it. Have you ever been flipped off by another driver and as they sped away in frustration, you noticed a faith-based bumper sticker on the back of their car? Has someone spoken down to you or ignored you altogether and you see a big ol' blingy cross around her neck? Have you heard a woman cussing like a sailor while sporting a *Be Kind and Love Jesus* T-shirt? But wait, there's more.

In college, my husband was a waiter. And the shift he hated the very most was the Sunday crowd because they were the worst tippers. What did that preach to him? I've seen faith-filled women flat-out drunk. . .more than once. I've seen hard-core Jesus-girls wearing the tightest, skimpiest clothes. . .in public. I've watched pillars of the faith fall apart when the curve ball hit, rather than walking out the faith they promote. And I've seen the questionable memes, hate-filled comments, and political rants Christians have shared on social media. I'll admit that I've been plenty guilty of these kinds of conflicting messages in my life. I bet you have, too. What are we doing?

Hear my heart on this. There is nothing wrong with having an opinion—even a strong one. It's okay to have righteous anger toward injustice. We all have moments of insanity. Everyone gets knocked down by life for a season. And standing up for those who need help or speaking out for certain causes is admirable. God gave you the ability to think and feel for a reason. But we can't forget that being *known* as a Christian means we're under scrutiny. I'm not suggesting we live one way at home and another in public. Nor am I suggesting that we need to always have it together. But if we want to have uncommon evangelism, we need to remember that our life preaches.

On the flip side, sometimes we choose to hide because we don't have the confidence to share Jesus. We become too scared to take an appropriate stand and end up sliding into one of these pits instead:

1) The pit of deception—we hide our faith so no one knows.
2) The pit of disregard—we turn a blind eye so we don't have to speak up.
3) The pit of dilution—we water down the truth so we don't offend anyone.

Rather than share Jesus with those around us, we shrink away from situations and opportunities. Instead of speaking up with truth, we keep our mouths closed. And when we do find the gumption to speak, we use words that are palatable and unopinionated. But God calls us to higher ground. Remember Matthew 5:13–16 that says we are the *salt-seasoning* and bring out the *God-colors* in the world. And when we accept this uncommon mantle, our life will point others to God. Friend, that's evangelism in a nutshell.

Priscilla

Priscilla lived those verses to a tee. She was a Christian Jew committed to spreading Christianity, and she and her husband traveled from city to city supporting Paul's ministry. As a matter of fact, when you read her story in the book of Acts, you'll learn she was recognized for helping build the early church.

Being a Jewish wife meant she was clearly under the authority of her husband. And at that time, only men were allowed to study God's law in the synagogue. The women would have been at home making meals, cleaning up, and raising kids. But you'll notice that both Priscilla and her husband Aquila are mentioned in Acts, and she is frequently mentioned first. That means something. No, she wasn't the traditional stay-at-home wife—not by a mile. Priscilla and her husband were not only partners in the trade of leather-making, but also partners in ministry.

This woman was an uncommon evangelizer for so many reasons! Her heart was burdened to further the Christian movement, and so she and her husband placed themselves on the front lines. They established a church in their home, often with her teaching and instructing. They traveled with Paul, supporting his critical ministry. And when his life was threatened, this couple gave Paul refuge in their own home because they knew his value to the movement. She was all in!

Priscilla may have never met Jesus in person, but her uncommon evangelism helped further the Gospel radically.

Lydia

Lydia was bold in her faith, too. A respected and affluent businesswoman in Philippi, she was a dealer in purple. Because she didn't have a husband, Lydia served as the spiritual leader of her home that included a number of slaves. And her house must have been huge as it hosted not only the church itself but the missionary party as well.

When we meet Lydia in Acts 16, she is a new believer. The Lord *"opened her heart"* after hearing Paul and Silas speak, and she (and her whole home) received the Gospel of Jesus. She became Paul's first convert in Europe and immediately invited the two to stay with her. And because he was confident that she was firm in her faith, he baptized her and accepted her invitation.

Lydia had a wide-open heart for Jesus, and she was on fire to share her enthusiasm with everyone who would listen. Oh, I love this next part. Since there wasn't a synagogue in the city, she decided to hold regular prayer meetings with other women by the river in Philippi. Can't you imagine the encouragement in the faith that happened by those waters? She was ready to do all she could to share the Gospel with others. The Good News transformed her, and now she wanted that same opportunity for others. That, my friend, is uncommon evangelism.

The Samaritan Woman

The Samaritan woman's story proves we don't have to be perfect and have it all together to evangelize. It also proves how powerful an encounter with Jesus can be. This woman—isolated, immoral, and considered worthless in the community—is credited for helping advance the Gospel in a region where it hadn't been heard yet.

We find this woman making her way to the well late one morning. The community's upstanding women had already filled their buckets and returned to town, and now it was clear for her to go. She always arrived in the heat of the day because it kept her from the judging eyes of others. But this one time, Jesus was there. And He asked for a drink.

What follows is the longest conversation between Jesus and an individual recorded in the Gospels. And as He unpacked parts of her life no stranger could have known, she became convinced that He was indeed the Messiah. It changed her.

John 4:28–30 says she left her water jug and ran back to town in hopes of convincing people to go see for themselves. The woman who for years had let guilt and shame keep her isolated now boldly testified in her community. The un-named woman tells everyone around the good news that she received from Jesus. And with her secrets exposed and hope restored, the power of her testimony caused many to believe (John 4:39)—a remarkable moment because in those days a woman's testimony was considered legally worthless. Verse 42 (NIV) says, *"They said to the woman, 'We no longer believe just because of what you said; now we have heard for ourselves, and we know that this man really is the Savior of the world.'"* She was able to reach her neighbors in a way that others in the faith hadn't.

These were ordinary, everyday women so moved by the Gospel—so moved by the love of Jesus—that they had to share it. Some were married and some single. Some wealthy, others not. One was in active sin and others upstanding citizens. And while they all preached with their words, their lives spoke just as loud—even the Samaritan woman. The community saw her newfound confidence in Christ as she boldly reached out to them.

Here's what I love the very most about the examples set by Priscilla, Lydia, and the woman at the well. In each story, their motivation was love. They didn't condemn, and they shared truth with kindness. They were uncommon evangelizers. And because of that, these three were recognized for advancing the message of Jesus. Oh let that be us!

Friends, we have to get this right because the world needs hope. And that hope is Jesus Christ. While the salvation of others is not our responsibility, pointing others to Him most certainly is.

So keep in mind that your life preaches. How you handle discouragement, disappointment, and doubt matters. The ways you celebrate others and how you respond to authority is noted. The way you talk about politics, race, sex, and religion makes an impression. The words you use, your facial expressions, and the way you act. . .it all matters. Your life preaches one way or another.

You're called to be an uncommon evangelizer. It's not about being perfect. It's about being purposeful. So let's remember that our lives speak just as much as our mouths do.

Lean into Him

Go out into the world and share the good news with all of creation. (Mark 16:15 voice)

But you must stay focused and be alert at all times. Tolerate suffering. Accomplish the good work of an evangelist, and complete the ministry to which you have been called.
(2 Timothy 4:5 voice)

And I pray that as you share your faith with others it will grip their lives too, as they see the wealth of good things in you that come from Christ Jesus. (Philemon 1:6 TLB)

"Keep open house; be generous with your lives. By opening up to others, you'll prompt people to open up with God, this generous Father in heaven." (Matthew 5:16 MSG)

"Staying with it—that's what God requires. Stay with it to the end. You won't be sorry, and you'll be saved. All during this time, the good news—the Message of the kingdom—will be preached all over the world, a witness staked out in every country. And then the end will come." (Matthew 24:13–14 MSG)

Look into You

What is your biggest barrier to evangelizing?

When have you seen effective evangelizing? When have you seen it ineffective?

Who are the people you'd like to share Jesus with? Write their names down. Brainstorm ways you can share truth with them.

What scripture or biblical character from this chapter speaks to you the most?

How are you going to have uncommon evangelism?

Live Uncommon

Lord, help me be a light in the world—not perfectly, but purposefully. Help my words and actions point others to You. Sometimes sharing my faith makes me anxious because the world is becoming intolerant. Would You give me the courage to evangelize anyway? Would You help me preach with my words and my actions? I am available to You and will walk through the doors You open. I want to be part of the reason Your name is praised in all the world. Please give me the boldness and confidence to not cower but instead stand strong as I praise my Father in heaven. In Jesus' name, amen.

CHAPTER 5

Uncommon Faith

So the impossible is possible with God.
Luke 1:37 VOICE

$\mathscr{W}$hen we say we have faith, it means we are choosing to believe in something or someone. It means we purpose to be loyal or true to a person or promise. It means we are devoted. We place our *trust* in it. And it's something we do without demanding proof. Faith is a big deal.

But the truth is, trusting doesn't always come easily. It may not be the same for you, but trust has been an epic struggle for me. Maybe it's because of the sexual abuse I suffered at the hands of a stranger when I was four. Maybe it's because my life has been filled to the brim with broken promises and violations. It might be because I became a control freak, trying to manage any potential pain that might be coming my way. I just didn't want another disappointment to tighten the *I'll-never-be-good-enough* tangles in my self-worth. So when I tell you trust has been a huge hurdle for me to overcome, I mean it. Maybe you know exactly what I mean.

Here's the problem though: You can't have faith unless you are willing to trust. They go hand in hand. Trust sets faith into action. And when you choose to have uncommon faith, you are essentially releasing control and placing your trust in God. It's believing that no matter what, He is capable and willing. And that's pretty easy to do until it all hits the fan. When we find ourselves overwhelmed with a situation, the choice to trust is so much harder.

Too often we cry out to God, *Show me first and I'll trust You second.* We are looking for confirmation that He's got our back. But God's response is a plea for us to have faith in Him. He says, *Trust Me now and then you'll see.* We want proof *from* Him. God wants our confidence *in* Him.

Listen, friend, we've all had days where we're sure we can't survive one more minute. Life can land a powerful sucker punch right in the gut that leaves us gasping for air. Marriages blow up, and dreams are shattered. Friends fail us, and our kids make terrible, life-changing choices. Finances dry up, health declines, and we lose people we love. Life is not fair. But uncommon faith means we trust God through it, because we know He is in it.

In the 1970s, there was an egg-shaped toy called a Weeble. (Wow, I feel really old right now. Bear with me, young'uns.) Looking at all the cool toys these days, the Weeble was actually pretty lame. But what made it a huge hit back in the day was that no matter how hard you tried to knock it down, it always came back to an upright position. It all had to do with the weighted bottom and gravitational force. My sister and I would try everything to knock it down and keep it down—but we couldn't. No one could. The marketing tagline was perfect: *"Weebles wobble, but they don't fall down."* This is a perfect mantra for uncommon faith.

Even when a sucker punch from life makes you double over in pain, you get back up. When your husband walks out, you get back up. When the doctor's report takes your breath away, you get back up. When your finances are strained, you get back up. When your best effort isn't enough to fix the situation, you get back up—just like a Weeble would.

Life will make you wobble because faith doesn't give you a free pass from hard times (John 16:33). And the pain may be so intense you'll want to crawl in a hole and die. We are human, and we will have human responses to the yuckies of life. But having uncommon faith means we don't stay down for long. It means our life is so weighted in Jesus that we always find our way back to hope.

We've probably all been the poster child for uncommon faith at some point. But if we were to be honest, we often have one foot in Camp God and the other in Camp Me. We may have every good intention to trust, but plan B is ready to roll if we don't get relief soon. And since His ways are not our ways. . .and His plans are not our plans. . .we struggle to wait in faith.

Friend, I want you to be *all in*. Your faith doesn't grow by chance but by choice. It's not a feeling but a fact. Every day you have to choose it. This is where the rubber meets the road.

This next statement is crucial because it's a heavy truth of uncommon faith. It's the foundational belief. And if we can cling to this, it will change everything. Ready? *God has a perfect track record in your life.*

Here's what that does *not* mean:
1) Life is pain-free.
2) Life is easy.
3) God will do what you want, when you want it.

Please, please, please unlearn these untruths. They are bad theology, and you would be hard-pressed to find any scripture in the Bible to support these claims. All too often, when people run into trouble and hard times—when help doesn't come soon enough, when prayers aren't answered in a specific way—it's the reality check that causes people to walk away from the faith. They think, *I tried it. It didn't work. I'm out.*

In contrast, here's what God's perfect track record *does* mean:

1) He has been intricately involved in every situation and every circumstance you have faced up to this very moment.
2) He has never abandoned you in hard times or left you to figure it out yourself.
3) He has answered every prayer the way you *needed* it to be answered, rather than the way you *wanted* it to be answered—and sometimes those were one and the same.

And from this point forward until you take your last breath, this track record will update real-time. The past tense verbs in these statements will become present tense verbs because God's role in your life is unchanging. He is active. He is faithful. He is reliable—then, now, and when.

If you can settle this in your heart and believe it when life gets intense, then you can be confident in your faith. You can trust that God is who He says He is. You can trust that God will do what He says He will do. And believing these truths will birth uncommon faith.

Faith is just like a muscle. Every time we trust God, we flex it. And the more we use that muscle, the stronger it will become. It will do the heavy lifting in dark times. But if we don't believe in God's sovereignty, our faith muscle will atrophy. It will become weak. C. H. Spurgeon says, "To trust God in the light is nothing, but trust him in the dark—that is faith."[3] That's uncommon faith, actually. And the only way for us to have that kind of faith is by letting God grow it.

Faith Grows through His Word

Romans 10:17 tells us faith grows through the Word of God. *"Yet **faith comes from listening** to this Good News—the Good News about Christ"* (TLB, emphasis mine).

This is why we go to church, listen to podcasts of sermons, read Christian living books, escape to weekend retreats or women's conferences, soak in worship music, and go to Bible study. We need to know His promises. We need to know what those before us experienced. And God uses it all to build our faith.

Faith Grows through His Hand

Luke 13:10–13 proves our faith grows when God moves in our life. *"Around this time, He was teaching in a synagogue on the Sabbath, the Jewish day of rest. A woman there had been sick for 18 years; she was weak, hunched over, and unable to stand up straight. **Jesus placed His hands on her** and suddenly she could stand straight again"* (VOICE, emphasis mine).

We hear powerful testimonies of redemption and healing, and it gives us confidence. We watch someone stand through the storms of life, and it gives us courage. We see God provide in unexplainable ways, and it gives us resolve. We feel the support of family and friends through hard times, and it gives us perseverance. It's when we're facing hard times that we need reminders that God is powerful and capable. And it gives us hope.

Faith Grows through His Children

Romans 1:11–12 says that faith grows through relationships with other believers. *"For I long to visit you so that I can **impart to you the faith** that will help your church **grow strong in the Lord.** Then, too, I need your help, for I want not only to **share my faith with you** but to **be encouraged by yours:** Each of us will be a **blessing to the other**"* (TLB, emphasis mine).

God created us for community because it fertilizes the soil that grows our faith. Simply put, we need to be around other Christ followers because they help us mature. They hold us accountable. They point us to God. They cover us in prayer. They speak truth and wisdom into our circumstances. They help us navigate messy situations. And while our common response to hardship is to hole up and go it alone—a reaction laced with fear, shame, and feeling like we just don't matter—community helps foster uncommon faith because we don't let insecurities keep us from asking for help.

My husband and I watched God use all three of these faith builders to repair our marriage on a collision course for divorce. Let me set the stage. We had married quickly, which didn't give us time to see the deep brokenness in each other—or ourselves, for that matter. We had so much baggage between us: addictions, abuses, trust issues, control tendencies, self-esteem struggles, and other gaping wounds. Of course we knew we had problems. Who doesn't, right? But we thought marriage and babies would fix them all. Oh to be young and naive. . .and delusional. I'll give you a second to stop laughing. Okay, ready for me to continue?

At that time, my faith was as common as it came. I only used it when I needed it, and I thought God was supposed to work *for* me. So when it all hit the fan, I filled His inbox with desperate requests to heal my marriage and waited for a miracle. Between attending church and going to small group, reading my Bible, and attending Bible studies, I figured I was doing all the right stuff. But I wasn't relying on faith. I was relying on formula.

Then God brought community. Now I have been in some amazing small groups, but there was one couples' small group in particular that helped grow our faith in profound ways. The church we attended was promoting small group sign-ups one weekend. Because we were new and desperate, we reached out to a group listed in the flyer—not realizing they were closed. And by an act of God, they welcomed us in anyway, completely unaware we were in the middle of a marriage crisis. What a divine setup!

When the small group realized the dire straits of our marriage, they intervened. They rallied around me and Wayne. The men met with my husband, speaking truth into him. The women met with me, listening as I shared my frustrations and fears. They prayed for us when we met as a group, and they took us to the throne room in their own prayer time. I've never seen community move in such a way. And it shifted our marriage.

The healing our group had been praying for began to happen right before our eyes. They saw it. We saw it. And soon, the light at the end of the tunnel looked more like a beacon of hope rather than a speeding train. Wayne and I had a renewed desire to make the marriage work. We decided to be part of the process rather than the problem and watched God move in unexplainable ways to heal our marriage—a marriage on the brink of divorce. And you know what it did? It built our faith and the faith of those around us.

Rebekah

We are introduced to a woman of uncommon faith in Genesis 24. Rebekah was a young girl of marrying age, probably in her early teens when she ran into one of Abraham's servants at the well outside of town. He was in this foreign land on assignment, searching for the perfect bride for Abraham's son.

Before he had finished praying and asking God to show him the young woman for Isaac, Rebekah appeared. She was hardworking and beautiful. And once God confirmed she was the one, the servant shared the reason for his journey with her brothers since their father was dead. They replied in verse 51 (NIV), *"Here is Rebekah; take her and go. . .as the LORD has directed."*

Hold the bus a moment. What would have been going through your mind had your brothers so easily given you away like that? Even though they asked for a ten-day delay to say proper good-byes, it might not have lessened the sting. But Rebekah was different. She was full of faith.

"So they called Rebekah and asked her, 'Will you go with this man?' 'I will go,' she said " (v. 58 NIV). She heard the servant's account of God giving him a sign that she was the one. Her father was Abraham's brother, so she was raised under his generational blessing. And because of the God-fearing home she grew up in, her faith was so great that she was willing to leave her home forever to marry a man she knew nothing about. That kind of faith preaches.

While others might have refused to leave their childhood home or say good-bye to the family that raised them, she agreed to go. More than anything else, she trusted God. And it was her uncommon faith in God's plan that was rewarded. Genesis 24:67 (NIV) says, *"She became his wife, and he loved her."*

Naaman's Wife's Slave Girl

In 2 Kings 5, we meet a nameless little maid who was captured as a child when the Syrians invaded Israel. She became a servant to the wife of Naaman, who was a highly regarded army commander suffering from leprosy. This infliction caused almost unbearable pain, and she knew it.

The scriptures reveal the slave girl felt compassion for Naaman. So she said to his wife, *"If only my master would see the prophet who is in Samaria! He would cure him of his leprosy"* (v. 3 NIV). When she told her husband what the girl had said, they got permission from the king and set out for Israel. They were on a mission to find the prophet Elisha. When he saw Naaman, he told the man to bathe in the Jordan River seven times. And it was through this healing that he became a follower of Jesus. Even more, many in his household gained a powerful testimony.

So many lives were transformed because of the little slave girl's faith. She knew healing was available to everyone— even the ones who took her from her home and family. Her confidence in the divine power of God's prophets makes her a young lady with uncommon faith. Her belief changed the trajectory of Naaman's life and family forever.

Friend, it's easy to have faith when everything is going as planned. But in an instant, everything can change. When the hard times hit—*and they will hit*—what kind of faith will you have?

You are being called out of ordinary, watered-down faith and into the kind of faith that takes you into the deep waters with God. He is faithful. He is trustworthy. And He wants you to anchor your faith to that truth so you can be. . . *uncommon.*

Lean into Him

Your faith, then, does not rest on human wisdom but on God's power. (1 Corinthians 2:5 GNT)

He replied, "God can do what men can't!" (Luke 18:27 TLB)

Removing action from faith is like removing breath from a body. All you have left is a corpse. (James 2:26 VOICE)

Then Abram believed in (affirmed, trusted in, relied on, remained steadfast to) the LORD; and He counted (credited) it to him as righteousness (doing right in regard to God and man). (Genesis 15:6 AMP)

Look into You

How would those closest to you describe your faith?

Think back to the last tough situation you faced. What kind of faith did you have through it? How would you change it for next time?

Who around you needs uncommon faith in what he or she is facing? Pray for him or her right now by name.

What scripture or biblical character from this chapter speaks to you the most?

How are you going to have uncommon faith?

Live Uncommon

Lord, I confess that trust is a struggle for me. You already know the reasons why I try so hard to be in control. Help me release those old hurts. And please forgive me for all the times I didn't trust You. I realize now that You have a perfect track record in my life. Thank You for that! You're faithful and reliable—now and forever. I want to be a woman of uncommon faith, and I want my faith to encourage the faith of others! Help me show my corner of the world the hope of Jesus! In His name, amen.

CHAPTER 6

Uncommon Forgiveness

*Forgive one another as quickly and
thoroughly as God in Christ forgave you.*
Ephesians 4:32 MSG

Of all the ways we are called to be uncommon, this might be one of the most important. And honestly, it's probably the very hardest to walk out. The problem is we can't seem to settle the *why-should-I*, so we find ourselves unable to release the offense and forgive the offender.

It's easy to live offended these days. It seems like everyone is ticked off at everyone. We're not politically correct enough. We don't promote racial and gender equality enough. We offend others by just praying to God. And for Pete's sake, even changing lanes on the highway seems to anger the driver we moved in front of. We are an offended society, and the undercurrent that keeps it flowing is unforgiveness. But let's talk about the struggle to forgive in our own little world.

While we run across mean-spirited people in our day-to-day lives, so often the ones who hurt us the most are in our circle of trust. These are the people we don't expect to injure us. Their betrayal digs deep because we let our guard down with them. We share our secrets and tether our heart to theirs. So when they wound us—either on purpose or by accident—we recoil. And within moments, bitterness sets in.

Maybe someone forgot your birthday or dismissed your

concern. Maybe your husband didn't notice your new hair color or the kids complained about dinner. Maybe a friend told your secret or Mom forgot to call you back. There are a million ways our feelings can get hurt, right? And rather than forgive and move on, we make them pay.

We give the silent treatment or make our responses short and biting. We make them work to get back into our good graces. We hold the offense over their head whenever we get the chance. And we even gather a team of supporters who make us feel justified in our pain. Oh, we can be nasty people when we operate in unforgiveness. These common responses are in the opposite direction of God's heart for us. He wants us to operate in uncommon forgiveness.

We may feel justified—because sometimes it feels good to hold on to grudges—but the truth is unforgiveness hurts you the most.

1) It hardens your heart, making it hard to almost impossible to love.
2) It fills your mind with anger, bitterness, or revenge.
3) It sabotages your self-worth, creating a victim-mentality scenario.

Even worse, it gives the Enemy a stronghold in your life. And when he finds a way to mess with you, he takes full advantage of it.

We all think forgiveness is a great idea until we have to do it. Hugs and handshakes give way to the claws and fangs. And I'd like to suggest it's because there are three lies the Enemy tells us that keep us stuck in unforgiveness.

LIE 1: *Forgiving Will Let Them Off the Hook*

When you forgive, it doesn't mean you're excusing that person for the way they hurt you. It doesn't even mean you're completely over what they've done. It simply means you are not going to let yourself be triggered by it anymore. It means you won't let what was done *to you* be bigger than what Christ did *for you*. It's not approving what happened; it's rising above it. Forgiving prevents their offense from destroying your heart.

LIE 2: *They Have to Apologize First*

This one could really trip you up. Think about it. What if you've lost contact with them, or the offender was a stranger? What if they've died? What if they don't even know they've hurt you? Even worse, what if they don't even care and have no remorse for what they've done?

This is big-girl-pants-wearing time. Because while waiting for someone to take responsibility for their actions and words is a worthy hope, it's an unrealistic expectation. Forgiveness has nothing to do with an apology. And if you cling to this lie, you could be plagued with unforgiveness for the rest of your life.

Author Robert Brault says this: "Life becomes easier when you learn to accept an apology you never got."[4] It's so true, friend. Because there is a good chance it will never come, and you have to decide to forgive anyway.

LIE 3: *If We Forgive, Then We Have to Forget*

Let's be honest—this is something only God is capable of doing. Seriously. When it comes to painful times, I have a very good memory. There are some offenses so intense I will never forget them. Chances are you're the same way.

Remembering a hurt doesn't necessarily mean you're holding a grudge. It could just mean that you are human with memories. And often, it's those memories that warn you of danger or protect you from further heartache. While we *can't* hold them over people we've forgiven, we *can* set healthy boundaries so they don't hurt us again.

I once heard it said that forgiving doesn't change the past, but it does change your future. This is some good wisdom right here. Let's stop believing the lies keeping us in the cycle of unforgiveness because it's making us ineffective. We're consumed with keeping the bitterness candle burning. And it's compromising our ability to be a good witness. Unforgiveness preaches loud.

Last year, I had to dig deep to find a way to forgive the betrayal of a friend. It wasn't that I lost just a relationship with her but the death of a ministry dream, too. One day everything was fine. The next day everything changed. The more I pursued her for clarity, the more she pushed me away.

Even now I don't know exactly what happened, but what I do know is that my heart broke. And that pain quickly led to a spirit of unforgiveness that almost took me out. It affected me so deeply. I knew I had to find a way to release the offense and get right with God. Only after processing it with a confidant and unpacking it with God was I able to move forward.

I'm not mad at her anymore. Instead, I'm sad for her. With so much turmoil in her life, she closed out some women who truly loved her. Her deep brokenness caused her to push away an opportunity to build something special. And even though I never got a real explanation or apology, I'm learning I don't need those things to forgive. Friend, neither do you. If we want to have uncommon forgiveness, then we need to stop believing the lies that entangle us.

But while forgiving others is hard, sometimes the one we need to forgive is God Himself. I completely understand this struggle. For most of my life, I was angry at God for allowing such evil to wind its way into my story. I unpack those details with raw honesty in my book *Untangled*. But let's just say my life has been anything but normal. Or easy.

Growing up, I struggled to justify the words in the Bible that said *God loved me*, especially with all the hard things He allowed into my life. And through some intense counseling, I discovered how very angry I was at Him. That's when the healing started.

I learned He never stopped loving me. He never stopped pursuing my healing. It's one of His greatest hopes for us. And little by little, I began to forgive God for not doing what I expected Him to do in my life. It's changed my life.

The Bible tells us God is good all the time. We read scriptures like Jeremiah 29:11 that remind us that God's plan is to prosper us. So to forgive God means we choose to believe He is good—even when His plan, His timing, and His ways don't make sense to us.

Remember our discussion about uncommon faith? Being a Christian doesn't guarantee an easy life, but it does guarantee that if God allowed it. . .it was only because it would benefit us and glorify Him. We don't have to know all the *whys* and *hows*; some things we won't know this side of heaven. We just have to settle this truth in our hearts and minds: *God is good all the time.* If we believe this, it will allow us to have uncommon forgiveness toward Him.

But we can't end our discussion on unforgiveness until we look at the one person who is often the hardest to forgive—*yourself.* And Eve is the perfect example.

Eve

This woman had it all—an amazing marriage, the ability to walk with God in person, and a beautiful and safe home. There was no conflict or competition or feelings of inferiority. She never knew the meaning of embarrassment, misunderstanding, hurt, calories, divorce, abuse, estrangement, envy, fear, bitterness, grief, disease, guilt, shame. Let's also assume there was no body odor, rogue chin hairs, or stretch marks either. Ha! Regardless, her life was perfect. But an Enemy entered the garden, and their encounter changed everything. You can read her full story in Genesis 2 and 3.

Eve allowed doubt to slither into her mind, and that led to the fateful decision that altered her world—and ours—forever. She bit into the apple. Adam took a bite. And then their eyes were opened, shame set in, fingers were pointed, consequences were given, and she and Adam were forever banished from the garden. Everything was great, until it wasn't anymore.

Can you imagine for a moment the sorrow she must have felt? As she looked over her shoulder while walking out of the garden, Eve saw her perfect life disappear. The intimacy she had with God, gone. Just think how very heavy the weight of guilt must have been on her shoulders. She and Adam would now realize the full human condition.

The relationship with God was forever different, a harmonious marriage with Adam was no more, and one of her sons eventually killed the other. How could she ever lift the burden of her choice in the garden off herself? While we don't know the process that got her there, it's apparent Eve found a way to forgive herself. It's that she found the strength to continue that proves it.

Many of us would have given up, crumbling under the weight of guilt and shame. Maybe you already have. But not Eve. She didn't become weak and wimpy. She didn't host a pity party. She picked herself up, dusted herself off, and moved on. Listen, if Eve could find a way to forgive herself for altering the entire world, you can find the courage to forgive yourself for messing up—even if it's a doozy.

A common response to blowing it is beating yourself up. But you are not common. No, you are an uncommon woman with the capacity for uncommon forgiveness. And it's one of the most courageous decisions you will ever make because when you extend mercy to yourself, it keeps you right with God. It closes the door to the Enemy's plan. And it helps keep your heart soft and fleshy. I know, I know. . .it's not always easy. It's rarely convenient. It's probably not even your default button. But it's so very necessary if you want to live and love the way Jesus does.

If we're going to be ambassadors of uncommon forgiveness, then let's choose to stop believing the lies and forgive. . .

1) when others offend us,
2) when we get mad at God, and
3) when we make mistakes.

Max Lucado says, "Forgiveness is unlocking the door to set someone free and realizing you were the prisoner."[5] Oh snap, this is so true. And if there is nothing else you take away from this chapter, I want this to stick. Ready? *Forgiveness is freedom.*

It means you are free from offenses. Free from consuming thoughts. Free to love completely. Free from a victim mentality. And free from bitterness. Now that is the kind of uncommon forgiveness I'm talking about.

Lean into Him

> *It does not hold grudges and will hardly even notice when others do it wrong.*
> (1 Corinthians 13:5 TLB)

> *"Never get revenge. Never hold a grudge against any of your people. Instead, love your neighbor as you love yourself. I am the LORD."*
> (Leviticus 19:18 GW)

> *At that point Peter got up the nerve to ask, "Master, how many times do I forgive a brother or sister who hurts me? Seven?" Jesus replied, "Seven! Hardly. Try seventy times seven."*
> (Matthew 18:21–22 MSG)

> *"But if you do not forgive others [nurturing your hurt and anger with the result that it interferes with your relationship with God], then your Father will not forgive your trespasses."*
> (Matthew 6:15 AMP)

Make this your common practice: Confess your sins to each other and pray for each other so that you can live together whole and healed. (James 5:16 MSG)

Look into You

Which of the three lies listed in this chapter do you listen to the most?

Who do you need to forgive? What has kept you from it? What will you do about it today?

What new idea or concept did God reveal to you through this chapter?

What scripture or quote spoke to you the most?

How are you going to have uncommon forgiveness?

Live Uncommon

Lord, help me offer mercy to those who have hurt me. Help me forgive You, if there is resentment built up. And Lord, if I need to forgive myself, please show me that, too. I confess that I've believed the lies of the Enemy, and they have kept me bound up in unforgiveness. I understand how unhealthy that is, and I want to be different going forward. I want to be an uncommon woman who lives in freedom! Would You help me be quick to forgive and quick to ask for forgiveness? I don't want anything to compromise my walk with You. In Jesus' name, amen.

CHAPTER 7

Uncommon Generosity

*If you see some brother or sister in need and have
the means to do something about it but turn a cold
shoulder and do nothing, what happens to God's
love? It disappears. And you made it disappear.*
1 John 3:17 MSG

"Hey, Carey, do you have a minute?" These words made
me turn around and walk back into the preschool office
where my kids were enrolled. "Sure, what's up?"

I was trying to be brave, but inside I was a mess. Just
a few weeks earlier, Wayne had been notified that he was
being laid off. Seventeen years at the same company, and
they were letting him go, along with hundreds of others. At
that time, we didn't have a lot of extra cash (not much has
changed), so this loss of income was a big deal. And having
both kids in private Christian preschool was probably the
luxury we'd have to do without until he landed another job.

The school secretary smiled at me and said, "I have
something to talk with you about. Is this a good time?"
Afraid she was going to remind me our payment was late,
I nodded slowly and sat in the chair in front of her desk.
"I'm excited to tell you that someone has paid your tuition
for the next three months!" I exhaled and burst into tears.
How could this be? After I pulled myself together, I called
Wayne and we cried together. We were both so surprised
and humbled that someone would dig into their pockets to

support us. We were deeply moved by this act of uncommon generosity.

The secretary never revealed who the donor was. At their request, they wanted to remain anonymous. Part of me was glad because I'm not great at receiving and would have felt indebted to the individual. She promised to pass along our gratitude, and we left it at that. My kids are teenagers now, and to this day I have no idea who stepped into our mess and blessed us.

What I appreciate the very most is the donor gave anonymously. Frank A. Clark says, "Real generosity is doing something nice for someone who will never find out."[6] Too often, people are generous out loud. They want to be recognized. It's an opportunity to stroke an ego or improve a reputation. Oh, I just can't stand it when giving becomes an opportunity to showboat. It's such a common response. God wants our generosity to come with the right motives.

Matthew 6:1–4 (MSG) reminds us that the world is not a stage. It reads:

> *"Be especially careful when you are trying to be good so that you don't make a performance out of it. It might be good theater, but the God who made you won't be applauding. When you do something for someone else, don't call attention to yourself. You've seen them in action, I'm sure—'playactors' I call them—treating prayer meeting and street corner alike as a stage, acting compassionate as long as someone is watching, playing to the crowds. They get applause, true, but that's all they get. When you help someone*

out, don't think about how it looks. Just do it—
quietly and unobtrusively. That is the way your
God, who conceived you in love, working behind
the scenes, helps you out."

I love The Message translation because the wording is so conversational. Sometimes reading scripture in different translations helps me understand it better. And this bit of scripture is one of the "in-your-face" passages to begin with. Put those two things together and we're left with three power-packed *don't statements* to keep in mind as we exercise uncommon generosity.

1. ***Don't** make a performance out of it.* If you crave a standing ovation or a round of applause when you give, chances are you're doing it for all the wrong reasons.

2. ***Don't** call attention to yourself.* If you feel the need to publicize who you're donating to or how much you're giving, consider those red flags of improper motives.

3. ***Don't** think about how it looks.* If you are hoping to be caught in action, wanting others to see your investment of generosity, your motivation might be corrupt.

Somewhere along the way, things changed. And while many of us still give from a pure heart, others of us have fallen prey to one (or more) of the *don't statements.* When did generosity stop being about helping someone and instead become a way to boost our status or self-esteem?

Here's what I mean. I heard a woman say out loud the dollar amount she was writing on her check at a fund-raising event. Someone else posted on social media every time his monthly charitable contributions posted to his account. I've even heard a woman complaining she'd have to wait on new furniture because of the huge dollar amount she and her husband gave to a charity. Seriously. That's just messed up.

Now hear my heart on this because it's important. *Sometimes we can't give anonymously, and sometimes we aren't supposed to.* Maybe the organization recognizes donors in their publicity. Maybe we hang pictures of our sponsored child on the fridge. Maybe we put our lake house in the charity's live auction. Maybe we sponsor a table at a fund-raising dinner. Maybe we write a check to a needy friend while we're sitting at coffee. Maybe we support our friend's daughter on a mission trip. These are beautiful ways to be uncommonly generous! In and of themselves, they are not bad or wrong. So how do we justify these based on the passage in Matthew?

I've learned that uncommon generosity is a condition of the heart, motivated by Jesus and with the hope of blessing others. It's a heart issue. So the question we have to ask ourselves is this: *What is the motivation for my generosity?*

When our tuition was paid, we were so grateful to our donor. But it was God who received the credit. While He is ultimately our provider, one way He takes care of us is through the uncommon generosity of others. So often we think of generosity in terms of financial gifts, but it can manifest in many different forms.

Be Generous with Your Resources

As I am typing this out, I'm at my sister's condo in the mountains for the weekend. I'm facing so many writing deadlines and needed some alone time to pound out ideas and words. So I left my family at home and drove three and a half hours into the Colorado mountains with a plan. It's been so fruitful. I've been able to rest, rejuvenate, clear my head, and write—all because Stefani was willing to share her resources. She may never know how much her generosity blesses me.

God gives each of us a different set of resources to share with others. When He prompts you to offer them up, others are blessed because it says, "You're worth my investment." For some, your generosity may be a much-needed answer to prayer. I know several families who prayed for a new-to-them car and one was donated, and I heard about a church member who gave their time-share to the pastor's family for a much-needed vacation. I've had gift cards show up in my mail when we were between jobs, and many times my coffee was paid for by the person in the car ahead of me. Every time someone invests in you, it is a reminder that God sees you. Be uncommonly generous with your resources, and bless others.

Be Generous with Your Time

The investment of time tells others how much they matter. Can you think back to a time when someone stood with you in the middle of your mess? They linked arms and helped you navigate through a difficult situation. It was exactly what you needed to get you over the hump. This is called the *Ministry of Presence*.

It's why we sit with our friend when her husband or child is in the hospital. It's why we help others move to a new home or help them paint the walls of the one they're already in. It's why we offer to watch their kids so they can have date night when the babysitter backs out. It's why we mentor the young wife when her marriage feels overwhelming. When you're uncommonly generous with your time—something we all selfishly try to protect—it ministers deeply to the receiver's heart. Be that kind of woman.

Be Generous with Your Love

I cannot begin to count the number of women I have met who were raised in a home where they never heard the words "I love you." I'd say I've met an equal number of women who don't even hear those words in their own marriage. And it breaks my heart for them, because knowing we're loved helps us thrive.

Being generous with your love means that you actually tell others you love them. It means you hug them and kiss them. It means you celebrate them—their birthdays, accomplishments, promotions, and engagements, and even the times they tried their hardest but failed. This kind of generosity can be a game changer.

So please don't be stingy or selective with your love. Be careful others don't have to earn it. Don't withhold it in your anger or disappointment. God is lavish in His love, and we should be, too. Take the time to learn how someone feels love, and then love them that way. Maybe it's words of affirmation or an act of service. Maybe it's touch or quality time. Everyone feels love differently, so generously love them in their way. Let's choose to be women who are uncommonly generous with our love. It will speak volumes to their hearts.

The Widow with the Two Coins

There is a beautiful story in Mark 12 about a woman who moved Jesus with her generosity—so much so, He prompted Mark to document his experience in verses 41–44.

Jesus was in the temple watching the crowd deposit money in the treasury. There were many wealthy people who threw in large sums of money, but then a widow showed up. She was the very poorest among them. But her heart was rich with love for God, and because of that, she willingly gave everything she had.

Without hesitation, she dropped her two copper coins—worth less than a penny—into the trumpet-shaped, metal receptacles. Can't you just hear the different sound her small offering made in contrast to the wealthy donors? Jesus certainly noticed.

He was so stirred by her uncommon generosity that He used it as a teaching moment for the disciples. "*The truth is that this poor widow gave more to the collection than all the others put together. All the others gave what they'll never miss; she gave extravagantly what she couldn't afford—she gave her all* " (v. 44 MSG). Her generosity was uncommon because it was purely selfless.

Mary Magdalene, Joanna, and Susanna

In Luke 8, we read about three women who traveled with Jesus and the others as they went from town to town sharing the Good News. Included in the party was Mary Magdalene, Joanna the wife of Chuza, who was the manager of Herod's household, and Susanna. Scripture says these three had been cured from evil spirits and diseases.

In The Message translation, verse 3 names these three women and then goes on to describe their generosity saying, *"who used their considerable means to provide for the company."* Luke doesn't elaborate or provide more details on what these *considerable means* are but reveals they gave substantially and significantly. It seems they were uncommonly generous with all they had. We see in scripture and in our own lives that so often, an encounter with Jesus can forever change a heart and awaken a generous spirit. I'd imagine the same was true for these women healed up by the Messiah.

I have a friend who experienced this kind of uncommon generosity, and her story is deeply moving. Several years ago, she and her family moved across the country, leaving a huge village of friends behind. This family of seven loved the Lord. They cherished each other and were pillars in the community. It was hard to see them go, but they wanted to be closer to his family.

Not long after moving, her husband committed suicide. No one saw it coming, and it left her alone to raise their five kids. I remember the exact moment she called me with the news. All I could do as I sat in the elementary pick-up line was scream at the top of my lungs. It was a tragic situation that stunned and saddened everyone who knew this family.

He was an amazing man who only loved God more than he loved his family. Being kind and generous himself, he was known to everyone as a great man. But depression distorted his perception of life and eventually took it. But what happened next was the most profound example of generosity I have ever witnessed.

Their couples' small group and others in the community

rallied around this family—a family they had only known for a short time. Every day she would come home to find prepared meals in the refrigerator in the garage. Women would come over and do her laundry and clean her home. People would continually stock her pantry with food. A group of men completed the half-done renovations upstairs. Her lawn was cut and the exterior of her home power-washed regularly. If there was a need, it was met.

Different families rallied around the kids, helping out with carpooling and emotional support. The church got involved and was very intentional to connect with each member of the family. Finances were covered. Counseling was provided. Support groups were opened. It was a beautiful thing to witness. But even more profound, their support wasn't only for a few weeks or months following his death. My friend and her kids were supported in these uncommonly generous ways for several years.

I once asked her if accepting the generosity of others was difficult. She replied, "It used to be very hard. But I learned that if I didn't say yes, it robbed them of an opportunity to be a blessing." Her statement is meaty, friends. It's rich with wisdom. And let's think about it for a moment.

What if Jesus had stopped the widow at the temple treasury and given her the two coins back, saying she should keep the money because rich people would make up the difference? What if Mary, Joanna, and Susanna were so moved by their deliverance, wanting to support the needs of the travelers, but Jesus said, "No thanks. We can manage." What if the school secretary shared the news about the caring donor covering our tuition and my response was, "We'd rather not take their money. We'll figure it out on our own.

Thanks anyway." What if my friend was too proud to accept the help of those around her and instead chose to manage that grieving household alone?

Now put yourself in the shoes of these people, hearts stirred with divine purpose and pure motives to be uncommonly generous. Think about the excitement they felt knowing they were going to bless someone with their resources . . .their time. . .and their love. And then imagine the disappointment and heartbreak they would have experienced had their generosity been turned down. That kind of rejection would have felt pretty lousy, huh? The point I'm trying to make is this: *let's not only be generous with our resources, but let's remember to be just as generous in our gratitude when others bless us.*

Let's be big-hearted women full of kindness. Let's be liberal in our generosity toward others. Let's give with the right motives, expecting nothing in return. And let's not be women who need to make a spectacle with our gifts and offerings. God has blessed us, and it's from that place of gratitude that we bless others.

More now than ever, God is calling us to keep the spirit of true generosity alive and active in the world. Because when we do, we'll be teaching the next generation to be uncommon, too. Let's do it together.

Lean into Him

> *Remember: A stingy planter gets a stingy crop;*
> *a lavish planter gets a lavish crop. I want each*
> *of you to take plenty of time to think it over, and*
> *make up your own mind what you will give.*
> *That will protect you against sob stories and*
> *arm-twisting. God loves it when the giver*
> *delights in the giving.* (2 Corinthians 9:6–7 MSG)

Don't forget to do good and to share what you have with those in need, for such sacrifices are very pleasing to him. (Hebrews 13:16 TLB)

This is my last gift to you, this example of a way of life: a life of hard work, a life of helping the weak, a life that echoes every day those words of Jesus our King, who said, "It is more blessed to give than to receive." (Acts 20:35 VOICE)

The whole congregation of believers was united as one—one heart, one mind! They didn't even claim ownership of their own possessions. No one said, "That's mine; you can't have it." They shared everything. The apostles gave powerful witness to the resurrection of the Master Jesus, and grace was on all of them. And so it turned out that not a person among them was needy. Those who owned fields or houses sold them and brought the price of the sale to the apostles and made an offering of it. The apostles then distributed it according to each person's need.
(Acts 4:32–35 MSG)

Look into You

What did generosity look like in your family as a child?

Take a minute and ask God to bring people to mind who need your generosity. Come up with a game plan to meet their needs—either on your own or with the help of others. Be a woman of action.

What keeps you from being more generous with your finances, your resources, your time, and your love? What can you do to change that now?

What scripture, biblical character, or personal story moved you the most? Why?

How are you going to keep uncommon generosity alive in your family or circle of friends?

Live Uncommon

Lord, I confess that sometimes it's hard to be generous. I can be possessive or selfish, wanting to hold on to what I have or protect my time. Please change my heart so I'm more willing to invest in others. Will You give me the motivation and opportunities to step out in faith and help when I'm needed? I want to have uncommon generosity so others are blessed. I want to be part of Your plan as You provide for others. I want to be all in! Thank You for all the times You've used someone's generosity to bless me. Now I want to be the one to bless someone else. Please use me, Lord! In His name, amen.

CHAPTER 8

Uncommon Gratitude

*Give thanks to God no matter what
circumstances you find yourself in.*
1 Thessalonians 5:18 VOICE

There is always something to be thankful for. Even in our darkest times, when it feels like life is crumbling around us, we can be grateful. When it seems hopeless, like nothing can change our bleak situation, we can always find something to appreciate. And when we choose to see the silver lining, it changes everything.

Gratitude is the lens that helps us focus on the positive. It turns our *not enough* into abundance and hopelessness into expectation. It brings clarity to confusion and perspective to chaos. It comforts us and ushers in peace. Without it, we will miss the fullness that life has to offer.

If you were to take inventory of your life, there would be countless reasons for you to be grateful. You have a roof over your head, a vehicle to drive, and food in the pantry. Every day you wake up to conveniences like electricity, clean water, and flushing toilets. You probably have more clothes in your closet than you need and can visit your favorite coffee shop or restaurant when the urge hits you. Chances are you have a great circle of friends and family who love and care for you. And you live in a country where laws are in place to keep you safe. Yes, you and I have every reason to be full of gratitude.

Miriam

Miriam—Moses and Aaron's protective big sister—did, too. She offers a beautiful example of uncommon gratitude through dance in response to God's goodness.

In biblical times, dancing was a way for people to celebrate happy events. It was an act of worship. And when you read about dancing in scripture, it's always linked to one of these two things. Miriam's leading of the Israelite women into dance is the very first mention of any dancing in scripture. And it was warranted because God had just closed up the Red Sea on Pharaoh's army. You can find the whole story in Exodus 14 and 15.

Few things spark gratitude more than being set free. And after four hundred years of slavery, being chased through the dry bed of the Red Sea and watching the death of a pursuing army served as a powerful catalyst for pure gratitude. No wonder a celebration broke out!

Exodus 15:20–21 (MSG) says, "*Miriam the prophetess, Aaron's sister, took a tambourine, and all the women followed her with tambourines, dancing. Miriam led them in singing.*" Their songs and dances demonstrated the gratitude of the entire community.

Haven't we all experienced God's mighty hand somewhere in our circumstances that led us to our own celebration of sorts? Diseases cured. Addictions removed. Families repaired. Hearts untangled. Relationships mended. Prodigals returned. Finances restored. God is so good to us, isn't He? And while finding gratitude in the good is easy, other times it's a bit tricky. It's much harder to find uncommon gratitude when there doesn't seem to be a reason for it. Yes, that is a different beast altogether.

Many years ago, I visited South Africa with my church and worked with women in the last stages of AIDS. One project we facilitated was creating memory boxes—something each woman would fill with family recipes, prized possessions, drawings, and personalized letters to be passed on to their children when they died. My mind had been prepped for the trip, but my heart wasn't prepared for the jolt it was about to experience.

I'd never seen such poverty. People were living in sub-human conditions, and it shocked me. We didn't work in the townships proper, but we spent enough time there to see the stark contrast between our world and theirs. It was a heart-wrenching reality check.

When I met the women for the first time, I choked back tears. Their beautiful black faces were filled with joy as they stared back at me. Their white teeth and eyes were so bright next to their dark skin. And although their clothes were ratty, it was obvious they tried to look their very best.

I worried the nature of the project might create a gloomy and somber atmosphere, but I was wrong. They chose gratitude, and it encompassed the entire room. It started with one woman humming, and others joined in. Another kept the beat by pounding on the table. And within minutes, they were all on their feet singing in full voice. Their harmony was amazing.

I sat in my chair and wept as they sang the most beautiful hymns, praising God with every word. Their lives were being robbed by a cruel disease and their children's fate unknown, yet they found reason to celebrate. That's uncommon gratitude, and that moment has been burned into my memory.

Here is the gold nugget to cling to: *choose gratitude anyway.* Listen, there are a million reasons *not* to be grateful. Every day, we face new letdowns and rejections. . .more bad news and scary situations. And too many of us are letting life pull us down. Stop it. Sweet one, you can do hard things, and that includes finding uncommon gratitude in the mess.

Do you know what the most powerful weapon in your arsenal is? Praise. And here is why it works.

1) *Praise Brings Perspective*

All day long I'll praise and honor you, O God, for all that you have done for me.
(Psalm 71:8 TLB)

When you thank God throughout your day, you are remembering His position in your life. He is hearing your gratitude for who He is. And you're letting God know that you recognize all the ways He has blessed you. But it does something for you, too.

It helps you realize that God is alive and active in your life every day. And because we are all prone to selfishness, praise takes the focus off you and your struggles and places it on God and His goodness. So when the hard times come, your heart will be too full with gratitude to drown in discouragement.

2) *Praise Brings Proximity*

Go through His gates, giving thanks; walk through His courts, giving praise. Offer Him your gratitude and praise His holy name. (Psalm 100:4 VOICE)

Praise brings you closer to God. Think about the connection you feel during worship. Can't it be a sweet time with Him? So often, it brings me to tears because I feel His presence thick around me. Maybe it does for you, too. Or maybe it's those moments when you're on your knees thanking God for intervening that make you feel closer than ever.

As His daughters, we praise our heavenly Father not because we have to, but because we want to be close to our Daddy. We love Him, and we need to know He is near. And it's in His presence that our gratitude is activated.

3) *Praise Brings Positivity*

O my soul, bless GOD. From head to toe, I'll bless his holy name! O my soul, bless GOD, don't forget a single blessing! He forgives your sins—every one. He heals your diseases—every one. He redeems you from hell—saves your life! He crowns you with love and mercy—a paradise crown. He wraps you in goodness—beauty eternal. (Psalm 103:1–5 MSG)

Praise is good for your soul because it ushers in a positive outlook on life. Instead of moping around or complaining about problems, spend the day recalling the goodness of God. Try it right now. Name five ways God has moved in your life, and then try to be the same ol' negative Nellie. You can't. Praise changes things for the better!

When you shift your focus, you'll become a more positive person because you'll have fresh reminders of amazing God-moments from your life. And that will make it easier to release your concerns into His capable hands again. Praise is a negativity buster and a gratitude generator at the same time.

Praise creates uncommon gratitude—pure and simple. Now that we know how to get it, let's dig a little deeper to see how it can also deepen your faith. Gratitude is essential to navigating the storms in life.

Gratitude and faith go hand in hand. That means if you're a Christ follower, then gratitude should be a natural side effect. But instead, so many of us Jesus-girls are walking around defeated and discouraged. Does that describe you right now? If you're feeling hopeless, unable to see the good in life, chances are your faith and gratitude are buried under a pile of life's mess.

Maybe life is really big right now. And rather than collect reasons for being grateful, you're overwhelmed with the messiness of a situation. Welcome to being human. Friend, I want to remind you of something really important, and it requires your participation. Ready? *Messy times are the most important times to ignite your gratitude.* Doing so doesn't discount your pain or ignore your concern, but there are real benefits.

It sticks it to the Enemy, who is trying to take you out of the game. It squashes the temptation to become self-centered. And it keeps your heart tender so you can be the salt-seasoning that flavors the world. You can be the reason someone sees the God-colors everywhere. Yes, gratitude is that powerful.

Mother Teresa once said, "The best way to show my gratitude to God is to accept everything, even my problems, with joy."[7] This is meaty. It's trust on steroids. And it is faith to the core. But just how can we be grateful for things like cancer? Or divorce? How do we find gratitude when we lose a loved one? When times are tough and nothing seems to make sense. . .when it feels like your prayers for healing and restoration are bouncing off the ceiling. . .when circumstances are not going the way you planned. . .your faith needs a powerful boost. Uncommon gratitude can do it.

I can think of several times where I've had to pray something like this: "God, I know You are in the details of this situation. I can't see You right now, but You promise to never leave me, so I know You're there. I trust that You are allowing this only for my benefit and Your glory. Thank You for being a big God, and thank You for having a perfect track record in my life!" Sometimes I prayed that in strength and sometimes in tears. Others times I was angry at God for allowing what He allowed, and I had to humble myself before Him. But every time I prayed it, something shifted in me.

Friend, we aren't thanking God for allowing cancer or death or pain. I'm not sure we could ever genuinely pray that. Instead, we are showing gratitude because we know God is bigger than what we are facing, and that He is intricately involved in the details. It's in the hard and hopeless places we have the perfect opportunity to deepen our faith roots. Because by doing so, He will sustain us.

Here's how I know that. Colossians 2:7 (TLB) says, *"Let your roots grow down into him and draw up nourishment from him. See that you go on growing in the Lord, and become strong and vigorous in the truth you were taught. Let your lives overflow with joy and thanksgiving for all he has done.*" Exercising uncommon gratitude reveals the depth of your faith. It honors God's position in your life. And it creates deeper fellowship with your Creator. It's a win-win-win.

So will you choose to thank God when life is overwhelming and hard? Will you find reasons to be grateful when struggling to catch your breath? Oh, please do. Please be that kind of woman. Thank Him for being God. Thank Him for promising to never leave you alone to figure life out by yourself. And thank Him that He will grow your faith through it.

Someone once told me not to focus on what's *lost*, but to focus on what's *left*. . .and to be grateful for it. That is sound advice that I'm now forwarding on to you.

Let's be women of uncommon gratitude. Let's develop it through praise and watch it ignite our faith. Let's not be seasonal or situational with our gratitude but instead be grateful to God no matter what. And let's show the next generation how it's done so they can harness its power in their own lives. I know you can do this. You have everything it takes to be uncommon. Now choose it.

Lean into Him

> *Be cheerful no matter what; pray all the time; thank God no matter what happens. This is the way God wants you who belong to Christ Jesus to live.* (1 Thessalonians 5:16–18 MSG)

> *Therefore, let us all be thankful that we are a part of an unshakable Kingdom and offer to*

*God worship that pleases Him and reflects
the awe and reverence we have toward Him.*
(Hebrews 12:28 VOICE)

*Oh, give thanks to the Lord, for he is good;
his loving-kindness continues forever.*
(Psalm 136:1 TLB)

*Remember what Christ taught, and let his words
enrich your lives and make you wise; teach them
to each other and sing them out in psalms and
hymns and spiritual songs, singing to the Lord
with thankful hearts.* (Colossians 3:16 TLB)

*Blessed be GOD—he heard me praying. He
proved he's on my side; I've thrown my lot in
with him. Now I'm jumping for joy, and
shouting and singing my thanks to him.*
(Psalm 28:6–7 MSG)

Look into You

What was your biggest takeaway from the discussion
on praise creating gratitude?

What are the barriers that keep you from developing
an attitude of gratitude in your life? Was a grateful
heart modeled in your home growing up? Are you
modeling it in your home now?

How do you feel about the relationship between faith and gratitude? What new revelation did the Holy Spirit reveal to you?

What connected with your heart the most in this chapter? Why?

How are you going to foster uncommon gratitude in your family or circle of friends?

Live Uncommon

Lord, thank You for showing me how vital gratitude is to growing my faith. I want to be all in! Would You please give me the spiritual eyes and ears to find Your goodness in my everyday life, as well as in those times where darkness is thick? Honestly, sometimes it's hard to look past my circumstances and see where You are. Remind me to praise You throughout my day so we stay connected rather than letting the hard times pull me under. Help me focus not on what was lost, but rather on what I have left. And help my attitude of gratitude be a model for others who need to know You are good all the time. In Jesus' name, amen.

CHAPTER 9

Uncommon Hunger for God

"You're blessed when you've worked up a good appetite for God.
He's food and drink in the best meal you'll ever eat."
Matthew 5:6 MSG

I was about to lose it. We were going around the circle
giving updates about where our hearts were, something I
usually love to do. I'm a deep waters kinda girl and always
ready to dive right in to feelings. But it had been going on
for hours, and there was bacon waiting for us. Bacon. And
as it was now approaching noon and brunch was in smelling
distance, my deep waters were drying up. I was becoming
hangry.

The Urban Dictionary defines *hangry* as when you are so
hungry that your lack of food causes you to become angry,
frustrated, or both—and the anger sometimes intensifies
into wrath. I love this word because it is spot-on, isn't it?
Can you remember a time you were so hungry that you
yelled at the kids, rolled your eyes at your husband, used
choice words on the driver who cut you off, or thought mean
things toward someone at work? Letting your need for sus-
tenance turn your happy into *hanger* is a real thing.

I'd like to suggest that we can become hangry on a spiritual level, too. The verse above tells us that God is the food
and drink of the *best* meal we'll ever eat. That's a bold statement. It's hard to imagine anything being better than queso
and chips from my favorite Texas food chain. And that's just

the appetizer! Think of your favorite meal, be it homemade or from a restaurant. Can you smell it? Taste it? Yum, right? Well the Word tells us God will satisfy and fill us up *even more* and *even better* than that scrumptious meal.

So it would make sense that if we can become hangry when we lack physical food, then we can most certainly become hangry when we lack spiritual food, too. And while foods like queso can tame our tummy, the only way to satisfy our soul is to gorge on God. But have you ever noticed how much quicker we are to fill our bellies with yummy food than we are to fill our hearts with spiritual food?

How many times have we said, *"Oh, I just need to find time to soak in His Word"* or *"My life is too busy to join that study, but I really need more Jesus"*? We've probably used an excuse like these too many times to mention, yes? So what keeps us from filling up when we're spiritually hangry?

Here are three common beliefs that keep us from developing an uncommon hunger for God.

1) *God's Plate Is Too Full*

Look at the state of the world. Natural disasters, radical terrorism, economic turmoil, racial tension, poverty, and starvation, and the list goes on. Sometimes it's easy to think God is too busy with more pressing issues so we should figure life out on our own.

We may be facing a diagnosis, but the Middle Eastern Christian is facing a beheading. Our finances are tight, but children in Africa are starving. Horrendous acts of hate are committed every day, and we decide they need God's attention more than our petty first-world strife. We're afraid to burden God with our pesky struggles because we feel there are bigger and more worthy issues in the world.

We may look back at our lives and the ridiculous choices we've made—or we consider our current season of sinning—and decide God should help those more holy. We think we've done it now—we've crossed the proverbial line—and it makes us afraid to ask for His help.

But when we believe this, we've limited God. We forget His plate is incapable of being too full, and He offers unlimited helpings of grace and love. He is available to you—to me—24/7/365. And no matter how shameful we feel, we can't ever escape His gaze or His goodness. No past, no sin, no fear, no insecurities, and no bad theology can separate us.

2) We Have to Feed Ourselves

In the world today, it's not considered cool to need people's help—much less God's. Marketing campaigns remind us we can do it *ourselves* or the answers are *inside us*. We decide being needy is a negative, so we don't ask anyone for help. When did vulnerability become a sign of weakness?

We read self-help books (this is not that kind of book) that promise to make us better. We go to conferences that empower us to be more. We keep our mouths shut when there's a call for prayer requests because we don't want to look pathetic. And when someone asks, "How are you?" our response is, "I'm good." But the truth is we're not.

It's in the dark of the night where we are battling the demons of loneliness and fear. And although we're exhausted from trying to hold it all together, we dare not share our desperate state.

Let me assure you that you were never meant to feed yourself. You're not required to figure it out on your own.

Asking for help when you need a fresh word spoken into your stale situation is not a negative. Remember, God created you to need Him and to crave community.

3) We Need Others to Feed Us

While it's true we were created to be part of a healthy community, it doesn't stop there. People are just one of the weapons in our faith arsenal. But somewhere along the way, we decided that others were the sole source of strength to help us navigate life. Not only did we stop believing in our own abilities, we began to doubt God's sovereignty in our lives, too.

I have great respect for the opinions and hard-won wisdom my friends and family can offer. I bet you do as well. But ultimately, God's voice must be in the mix. His voice needs to be louder than yours or theirs. God never created *them* to replace *Him*. If God is the cake, then others are the sweet icing that tops it.

Having an uncommon hunger for God is a product of our intentionality. It doesn't happen by chance. That means attending church once in a blue moon or only going to Easter and Christmas services won't create it. Wearing a faith-based T-shirt to coffee or posting a scriptural meme on social media is great, but alone it won't cultivate an uncommon hunger for God. And you can't ride in on the coattails of your spouse's faith or your parents' faith, hoping to benefit from their relationship with Jesus. It doesn't work that way.

What I want to share next is a hard truth. And understanding it will help usher in the uncommon hunger for God we need to thrive in a world that can be so dark.

Ready? Here it is: *we need to want God more than we want anything or anyone else.*

More than status; more than money; more than a reputation; more than justice; more than a husband; more than children; more than that job; more than food; more than the advice of others. We must want God *even more*.

That means when the bad news comes, we plop in His lap rather than grab chocolate. We take our pain right to Him instead of expecting friends and family to make everything better. We let God fight for us rather than picking up an offense and plotting revenge. We step back and let God protect our name. It means we choose Him over everything else the world has to offer.

Relying on anything other than God will do nothing but keep us in an ordinary, common relationship with Him. We will have all of His power and strength and wisdom available to us, but we'll settle for the world's offerings instead. And when we choose the world over God, that choice will starve us spiritually.

Let's be honest, though. When we find ourselves in crisis and chaos, we're desperate for immediate answers. And because we have a brain and are resourceful, it's not hard to come up with immediate solutions to our situations. But did you think to ask God about His remedy? If you're serious about cultivating an uncommon hunger for God, choose to want Him more.

Mary of Bethany

Mary had that kind of hunger for Jesus. If you remember the story from Luke 10 when Jesus and company had stopped at the house she shared with her older sister Martha,

Mary decided to sit with the Messiah instead of help in the kitchen. This was a very risky move!

In that culture, being hospitable was almost a sacred duty and something Martha took great pride in. But Mary abandoned her sister in the middle of food prep because she decided she wanted Jesus more. The eldest then went to Jesus, asking Him to intervene and reprimand Mary for leaving her all the work. His response drives home my point.

In Luke 10:42 (MSG), He affirms her decision by saying, *"One thing only is essential, and Mary has chosen it—it's the main course, and won't be taken from her."* Mary's choice of Jesus over cultural protocol was a powerful show of uncommon hunger for Him.

She showed her adoration for Jesus another time when she emptied an alabaster jar full of very expensive ointment onto Jesus' feet as He was eating dinner in the house of Simon the leper. The disciples were furious. They knew her perfume was worth a lot and would have been used to help the poor. He spoke up, and in Matthew 26:10–13 (MSG) responded to them by saying, *"Why are you giving this woman a hard time? She has just done something wonderfully significant for me."*

Mary was so extravagant in her hunger for Jesus that He went on in that same passage to say, *"What she has just done is going to be remembered and admired."* Time and time again, her uncommon hunger for Jesus replaced the opinions and ideas of others.

The Woman Who Lived a Sinful Life

Like Mary of Bethany, this woman wanted what Jesus had to offer over anything else. Her beautiful story unfolds in

Luke 7:36–50. She was most likely a prostitute or adulteress, living a notoriously sinful life. But what she did proved her uncommon hunger for Jesus was stronger than her desire for the life she'd been living.

When she heard He was in town, she picked up her expensive alabaster jar of perfume and found Him. There she stood in His presence, crying. Her tears fell onto his feet. And verse 38 (MSG) says, *"Letting down her hair, she dried his feet, kissed them, and anointed them with the perfume."* I can feel her desperation, can't you?

By washing His feet, she did the act reserved for the lowest, most inexperienced servant in the home. But she wanted Jesus more than her pride, more than her costly perfume, and so much more than her sinful life. Then Jesus said, *"I forgive your sins."* And her uncommon hunger for Him changed her life forever.

The Bleeding Woman

This story speaks the loudest to me because I've been at this point so many times in my life. I know what it feels like to be at the end of *you* and in desperate hunger for *Him*.

In Mark 5, we meet a woman who had been bleeding for twelve years straight. Twelve years, friend. No break. No reprieve. Just the constant issue of blood for twelve long years. This condition—which she did not cause or ask for—labeled her as a *defiler* by society. Let me show you why.

Leviticus 15:25–27 (TLB) reads:

> *"If the menstrual flow continues after the normal time, or at some irregular time during the month, the same rules apply as indicated above,*

*so that anything she lies upon during that time
is defiled, just as it would be during her normal
menstrual period, and everything she sits on is
in a similar state of defilement. Anyone touching
her bed or anything she sits on shall be defiled,
and shall wash his clothes and bathe and be
defiled until evening."*

No way around it—bleeding was offensive.

Every day for twelve years, she would have defiled her bed and anything she sat on (chair, rug, stool, garment, etc.). Not only that, anyone who touched these "defiled" things was considered defiled as well. No one would have wanted to keep her company because of the cleansing process they'd have to complete once they left her home. And no one would invite her to gatherings for the same reason. So for all intents and purposes, she was a social outcast.

Who would have comforted her on a bad day? Who would have spent holidays with her? Who would have celebrated her birthday? Can't you just imagine how badly she wanted to be healed? Not only was she considered unclean and unaccepted in social settings, but this condition probably left her weak and sickly. Verse 26 tells us she'd seen countless physicians who treated her badly, many taking her money and leaving her worse off than before. But then she heard about Jesus.

Pushing her way through the crowd, she wanted Jesus more than worrying about defiling others. She had uncommon hunger for what she believed He could offer her. She thought, *"If I can just put a finger on his robe, I'll get well"* (v. 28 MSG). And the passage goes on to tell us that's exactly what happened. The moment her hand touched His garment, the bleeding stopped. She was healed.

These three women offer us beautiful reminders of what it looks like to hunger for God. What made it uncommon? They were desperate enough to reject societal values and cultural stereotypes to have an encounter with Him. They thought out of the box with their faith. They realized He was their only hope. And they wanted Jesus more than anything else.

How do you and I create that kind of appetite for God in our own lives? Here are three ways to make us hungry.

Spend Time in the Word

If you are not in the Word every day, you are spiritually starving yourself. A friend used to ask me this question when I was cranky: *When was the last time you opened your Bible?* And as annoying as that question became (because I was in a season where she had to ask me all the time), it opened my eyes to the reality of hangry. For me—and maybe for you, too—there's a direct connection between feeling hopeless and being easily frustrated and not spending time in the Bible.

We may have every good intention of finding sacred space to open the Word, but we just don't make it happen. And for whatever reason, our Bibles sit and collect dust. But when we invest the time, we're never disappointed. If you want to have an uncommon hunger for God, then digging into the scriptures every day will get you there.

Spend Time with Other Hungry Believers

We've already talked about how awesome—yet tricky—

community can be. But the truth is, surrounding ourselves with other hungry believers keeps us at the table. Hebrews 10:25 (GW) says, *"We should not stop gathering together with other believers, as some of you are doing. Instead, we must continue to encourage each other even more as we see the day of the Lord coming."*

I always appreciate coffee dates where God is the main topic of conversation. If the discussion turns to recipes or fashion or the latest reality TV show, I often look for an excuse to leave. But if we chew on the latest sermon or where He is moving in our lives, I'm hooked. When we ask tough questions about theology and dissect it together, I'm all in. If my friend wants to unpack faith and suffering and forgiveness, it jazzes me up. It's meaty, and I love every minute of it. But you know what it does for me the very most? It encourages me to go even deeper with God. And I need that. *We need that.*

Connecting with women who love the Lord fast-tracks me to a new level of hunger for God. It creates an uncommon desire to go deeper.

Spend Time in Prayer

This feels like a "duh" statement. Everyone knows the key to any good relationship is communication—the kind where you talk often and with purpose. And many of us have seen the devastating effects of what happens when we don't. Talking to God is an essential part of developing an uncommon hunger for more of His presence.

Too often, we make prayer harder than it has to be. We turn a personal conversation into a graded presentation. We worry if our words are right. We try to use big, flowery sentences so we sound more holy. Rather than just talk, we get caught up in making our prayers lofty. And too often, we focus on the mechanics of the prayer instead of the heart of the prayer itself. Don't do that. Remember, God isn't looking for the perfect prayer. He wants purposeful ones. Just talk to Him.

You also don't need to be in the perfect setting to pray. Geez, I pray all day long. Not a constant streaming of words, but I will just acknowledge Him when it seems right. It might be, *"Lord, please give me wisdom here"* or *"Father, help this conversation go well"* or *"Thank You for a close parking place since it's raining!"* Carving out quiet time is great, but don't forget to include Him in the rest of your day, too.

Having an uncommon hunger for God is something we have to cultivate. The idea is that God becomes our default button. He is our first stop when the crazy train starts to leave the station. He is the one we crave instead of reaching for the short-term fixes the world has to offer. Friend, I want you to want God more than anyone or anything else. In the depths of your DNA, I want you to believe your strength comes from Him alone. And I want to give you permission to be *that* crazy Jesus-girl.

Be like Mary, who was willing to risk reputation to soak in His presence. Be like the woman who lived in sin, understanding the real value is Jesus—not anything of the world. And just like the woman struggling with blood, ask God for healing and restoration. Because when you do. . .you'll develop an uncommon hunger for Him. And it will change your life.

Lean into Him

*"Now pay attention; I am standing at the door
and knocking. If any of you hear My voice and
open the door, then I will come in to visit with
you and to share a meal at your table, and you
will be with Me."* (Revelation 3:20 VOICE)

*So let God work his will in you. Yell a loud no to
the Devil and watch him scamper. Say a quiet
yes to God and he'll be there in no time. Quit
dabbling in sin. Purify your inner life. Quit
playing the field. Hit bottom, and cry your eyes
out. The fun and games are over. Get serious,
really serious. Get down on your knees before the
Master; it's the only way you'll get on your feet.*
(James 4:7–10 MSG)

*"If God gives such attention to the appearance
of wildflowers—most of which are never even
seen—don't you think he'll attend to you, take
pride in you, do his best for you? What I'm
trying to do here is to get you to relax, to not be
so preoccupied with getting, so you can respond
to God's giving. People who don't know God
and the way he works fuss over these things,
but you know both God and how he works.
Steep your life in God-reality, God-initiative,
God-provisions. Don't worry about missing
out. You'll find all your everyday human concerns will be met."* (Matthew 6:30–33 MSG)

"I love those who love me. Those eagerly looking for me will find me." (Proverbs 8:17 GW)

I have thought much about your words and stored them in my heart so that they would hold me back from sin. (Psalm 119:11 TLB)

Look into You

What was your biggest takeaway from the discussion on being spiritually "hangry"?

What is the obstacle that keeps you from filling up those empty places inside with God?

How would you describe your desire for God right now? What can you do to want Him more?

What woman from the Bible did you connect with the very most in this chapter? Why?

How are you going to foster an uncommon hunger for God within your family or circle of friends?

Live Uncommon

Lord, help me want You more than I want anything else. It's so easy to get hangry and look to the world to satisfy my needs or heal my heart. But in doing so, I'm forgetting that You are my provider. You are ready and willing and able to be my all. Help me choose You! I don't want to live a common life. Instead, I want to thrive as an uncommon woman who is completely sold out for You. Forget the world. I want You! In Jesus' name, amen.

CHAPTER 10

Uncommon Kindness

When she speaks, her words are wise,
and kindness is the rule for everything she says.
Proverbs 31:26 TLB

I'll be honest: I used to think kindness was a mark of weakness. In my mind, strong people were bold and kind people were spineless. They were doormats. And even more, they were wimpy. I considered being nice a sign of inferiority and so I chose to be hard instead. That plan didn't score big points with my family or friends, but the last thing I wanted to be known as was a wet noodle. Oh to be young and foolish. Friend, I was so wretched in my younger years.

But then I would see women I admired being considerate in response to someone being rude, and I began to recognize the strength it took not to blast them back. I'd watch as they were gentle when responding in a heated situation instead of defending their position with force. I'd see compassion for those who were hurting in place of an *I-told-ya-so* mentality. And I was convicted. I was convinced it actually took real courage to be kind. In the end I decided that kindness wasn't cowardly at all.

When God added kindness to the fruit of the Spirit listed in Galatians 5:22, He did so because it was a characteristic worthy of receiving. It was a gift—a good thing. And according to our Creator, it was something He wanted us to be able to access through Him. Some translations call kindness by a different name. For example, The Message translation refers to it as a *"sense of compassion in the heart"* and the King James translation lists it as *"gentleness."* And even the Matthew Henry's Commentary describes it as a "sweetness of temper."[8]

The problem is that so few of us are operating in kindness today. In our minds, we have good reason to act like we do—bothered, aggravated, and put-out. Sometimes it's as simple as the fact that we believe we're better than others. Like what we are called to do is somehow more important. We decide we are smarter, have more clout, are more known, our time is more valuable, or a million other things. We give ourselves permission to act as if we're *better than* they are. So we decide being kind is beneath us, and we become dismissive or easily annoyed. And it's ridiculous.

Lacking kindness could also stem from deciding someone doesn't *deserve* our kindness. I've seen people look preposterous in restaurants because their food came out late or the order was wrong. Even when the server and manager did all they could to fix the situation, the patrons were inconvenienced and wanted everyone to know it. I've watched people huff and puff and roll their eyes because the person at the front of the line was taking longer than they thought was necessary, making it painfully obvious they were bothered by their lack of speed. And rather than walk out our faith and extend kindness, too often we extend exasperation. We send the message loud and clear. . .something so common to the world today.

Other times we decide to play judge and jury and make others pay for aggravating us. When they make us angry, hurt our feelings, mess with our kids, spread rumors, or take the wrong side of an argument. . .we sentence and execute their punishment with precision. In our version of reality, they are undeserving of our time and attention. And even when they sincerely apologize, we withhold forgiveness and kindness.

But one of the most frustrating things I see is being kind with motives. It's putting on your best behavior so you'll get something in return. Once I received a book from an author who wanted me to help promote it during the launch. Launching a book is a big deal and takes a lot of time and effort, something I've done to help authors many times before. But she needed my help right in the crunch time of my own book writing, and I didn't feel I could give her launch the attention it deserved.

I was surprised when her entire demeanor toward me changed because I had to decline the invitation. One day she was solicitous and friendly, and the next she was cold. I don't pretend to know the depths of her heart, but for me it felt like she was kind for one reason only. And when she didn't get what she wanted, she showed her true motives. She was kind with expectations. Unfortunately, it's pretty common.

We have to be so aware of our motivation. Sometimes we use kindness as a way to make us feel better about ourselves. To appease the guilt and shame that tangles up our self-worth, we gush kindness. It's a selfish desire because we want others to affirm that we are good. We aren't being kind for their sake; we're being kind for our own.

I'll be honest, I can think back to times in my life where I've misused kindness. I've actually been guilty of every one of the ugly things I've previously described in this chapter. Chances are, you have, too. The combination of our human condition and the way of the world can sometimes get the best of us, which is why uncommon kindness is only accessible through Jesus. We need Him to empty our heart of selfish motives and fill it with selfless intentions. It's what needs to happen if we're serious about being salt-seasoning and showing others the God-colors in the world.

One of my favorite quotes is this: *Of all the things you can choose to be, choose to be kind.* I can't remember where I heard it, but it stuck with me. It's a message I try to drive home with my kids, too. You see, kindness is most certainly a choice. Knowing you have options and choosing kindness anyway takes courage. It's a bold move. And it's uncommon.

Think back to a time when you were a royal stinker to your husband, or when you betrayed a friend's confidence. Think of when you messed up at work or made a huge mistake with one of your kids. Now contrast the difference between when they responded to your blunder in kindness versus when they responded in anger and annoyance. One allowed grace to flood in to the situation while the other brought forth all sorts of guilt and condemnation. Yes, kindness can shift the entire situation.

I've seen it disarm anger, soften prejudice, change hearts, renew relationships, settle anxiety, calm circumstances, and promote peace. No wonder God includes it in the nine fruits of the Spirit. He wants us to use it with great intentionality.

The *Zondervan NIV Bible Commentary* says the word *kindness* used in Galatians 5:22 in Greek means "the divine kindness out of which God acts toward humankind. It is what the [Old Testament] means when it declares that 'God is good,' as it so frequently does. Christians should show kindness by behaving toward others as God has behaved toward them." This means we act with compassion and thoughtfulness toward others because God has acted that way toward us. We have the ability, but we have to choose it.

We've all heard the term *random acts of kindness*, and maybe we have experienced it firsthand. It's essentially a selfless act performed out of kindness to encourage a total stranger. It's something done in hopes of making others happy. A couple of times, the person in the car ahead of me has paid for my coffee, and thoughtful gifts have shown up in the mail from *anonymous*. It's a quick way to put a smile on my face! And it's an uncommon way to bless others, too.

So here's a challenge. Let's be women who make these "acts" more deliberate than random. Let's show uncommon kindness by sending a snail mail note to someone who needs to know they matter. Maybe take yummy food to the police precinct in your area. Go ahead and purchase the drink or meal for the person in line behind you or drop off a thoughtful gift for no special reason. Take homemade bread to your neighbors, write notes to missionaries, compliment how nice people look, hold the door open, clean up someone else's mess, give someone your seat, offer to carry groceries, mow someone's lawn. But let's not stop there.

You can choose to be kind with your responses to others, too. When you want to respond snarky or growl a response, when you want to act annoyed or rub it in, when you want to speak your mind or sit in judgment—choose to be empathetic and kindhearted instead. You can share your hurt feelings and put boundaries in place without losing your cool. You don't have to be mean to be firm. With God's help, you can show uncommon kindness through your words and actions. It's a choice you get to make every day.

Pharaoh's Daughter

This courageous and compassionate woman was credited for saving a chosen baby boy from certain death. Without knowing it, she protected Israel's great deliverer—Moses. Her father had created an edict to drown all newborn Hebrew babies. It was an Egyptian plan to control the Israelite population. In his fear of potential rebellion, Pharaoh decided to murder innocent children. You can read the details in Exodus 1 and 2.

When her maid returned with the basket she had seen floating in the Nile, she opened it to find Moses crying. Exodus 2:6 (VOICE) says, "*Her heart melted with compassion.*" The princess was smitten. Her heart was stirred with great love. And because of it, she risked her father's anger and wrath by choosing to keep the infant. Without intending to, she was showing uncommon kindness not only to Moses himself, but also his family and the entire nation of Israel.

She could have easily turned this Hebrew baby over to her father or drowned him herself. She could have put him adrift again. But unlike her father, her heart wasn't hard. It was still fleshy and full of compassion and kindness. And even though she wasn't being purposeful in saving Israel's deliverer, she did know she was saving a Hebrew baby. She was full of sympathy, not prejudice. She was driven by benevolence, not discrimination. And she cared enough to save this tiny human regardless. That is uncommon kindness.

Dorcas (a.k.a. Tabitha)

Dorcas lived in Joppa, a town on the Mediterranean coast about thirty-five miles west of Jerusalem. She was a widow but didn't sit and sulk. Instead, she found purpose by serving and blessing others.

Belonging to one of the earliest Christian congregations, she was deeply loved and respected by them. Dorcas was filled with uncommon kindness and showed it in very practical ways. Verse 36 of Acts 9 says she was *"a believer who was **always** doing **kind things** for others, **especially for** the **poor**"* (TLB, emphasis mine). I imagine she cleaned and cooked for others, sewed new garments, mended their old clothing, and met the countless needs of her community. But she soon became sick and died.

Full of desperation and hope, her friends went to fetch Peter, who was close by in Lydda. He returned to Joppa with them and went into the upper room where her body lay. I love the picture painted by verse 39. It reads, *"The room was filled with weeping widows who were showing one another the coats and other garments Dorcas had made for them"* (TLB). They were not only mourning her death but celebrating her legacy of kindness, too.

In the next verse, Peter commanded her to rise. In that moment, her eyes opened and she sat up. He took her hand, and he helped Dorcas to her feet. This resurrection became known all over Joppa, and verse 42 (TLB) says, *"And many believed in the Lord."* Not only did her acts of kindness speak volumes about the love of Christ, but so did her very life.

Dorcas wasn't seeking a loud and powerful ministry—one where she was known. She just wanted to love others the best she could. She wanted to be the hands and feet of Jesus. And her gift to the community was a selfless heart willing to fill a need. She was faith in action. Dorcas demonstrated uncommon kindness to everyone around her.

We sure could use some more kindness in the world. Here are five reasons why we need to be kindness carriers:

1) *It's Contagious*

Kindness is self-replicating. Think about it. When someone is kind to you, it tenders your heart and makes you want to pass it along. That means you have the unique ability to encourage others to demonstrate uncommon kindness, too. The more we show kindness, the more kindness spreads into the lives of others.

I mentioned this earlier, but it's the perfect illustration for here and now. When someone ahead of me purchased my coffee in the drive-through, I ended up purchasing the coffee for the car behind me. Kindness breeds kindness.

2) *It Strengthens*

Because there will always be sorrow, we will always need kindness. Bad news will always come, diseases will always rob us of life, relationships will always struggle, which is why kindness is always so important.

When I was diagnosed with cancer in 2010, my community flooded me with kindness. Knowing that I was loved kept my spirits high. Watching people care for my family spoke peace into my fear. And every note, phone call, delivered meal, and gift gave me the strength to fight through depression and discouragement for another day. Kindness matters.

3) *It's Free*

Being kind is something we can all engage in—anytime and anywhere. And it doesn't require you to spend a dime. Compliments are free. So is helping a friend move, holding open a door, creating a homemade card, or sitting with someone in the hospital.

My friend sat with me while an IV needle was inserted into my arm for a procedure. You'd have to know how desperately afraid of IV needles I am to fully understand how much her presence spoke to me. It's an irrational fear, I know. But having her there enabled the nurse to get it in successfully. It cost my friend nothing but a sore hand as I squeezed it tight.

4) It Makes a Difference

Every day presents new opportunities to show kindness. By just keeping your ears and eyes open, you will begin to recognize someone's need for help. From encouraging through a note to bringing a meal to helping someone carry a load, kindness is seeing and acting in a compassionate way. The end result is making someone feel valued and worthy of your time and effort. And who doesn't need that message reinforced from time to time?

When we moved a few years ago, we were bracing to spend a pretty penny to get our stuff to our new home. There was so much to move. A friend offered to gather a few from her church community to help, and for the entire day these amazing twentysomethings hauled beds, sofas, tables, and boxes. They asked for nothing in return. When my father asked them why they were so generous with their time, one woman replied, "Because that's what we do when we love Jesus. And now Carey and her family will pay it forward."

Their kindness saved us thousands of dollars and filled our hearts with the truth of how much God loves us. We'll never forget it, because it made a huge difference.

5) *It's God's Will*

Proverbs 19:17 (VOICE) reads, *"Whoever cares for the poor makes a loan to the Eternal; such kindness will be repaid in full and with interest."* This means when we show kindness to others, we're also showing kindness to God Himself. It doesn't go unnoticed. And even more, we will be blessed because of it.

The poor in this verse doesn't necessarily mean just those lacking in finances. We can be poor in a myriad of ways. Many are broken in spirit, weak at heart, and feeble in health. Aren't we all poor somewhere in our life and need the kindness of another? Phone calls, e-mails and notes, big bear hugs, a favorite coffee drink, a listening ear. . .these intentional acts of compassion can encourage someone like nothing else. No wonder it is part of God's will.

But I want this next statement to sink in deep because it's so important. You may want to grab your highlighter for this one. Ready? *One of the most important people you need to be kind to may be. . .yourself.* Because too often, you're using your own words to beat yourself up. And it's just not okay anymore.

Why are we so hard on ourselves? We're quick to extend grace to others but not to ourselves. Aren't we all doing the best we can with what we have and then asking Jesus for the rest? Bullying ourselves doesn't help. Here's what I mean.

As I am writing this section, my husband is prepping to go in for knee surgery this afternoon. The meniscus is torn and needs repairing. Because life and work have been so hectic, he forgot that ibuprofen wasn't allowed four days prior to surgery—and he'd been taking it. When he discovered this oversight last night, he freaked out.

Rather than taking a deep breath and giving himself grace, he began calling himself names. Stupid. Idiot. Moron. He was verbally berating himself. More than anything, it was discouraging to think his surgery might have to be rescheduled. My man is tired of the pain. But his words were unfair because he is amazing and deserving of his own grace and compassion. Having uncommon kindness means we treat ourselves with respect first. And it's out of that sense of worth and asking Jesus for help that we can be compassionate to others.

Let's choose to be women of kindness. Let's be intentional to leave a legacy of compassion. Let's be known for having big hearts. And let's remember that when we live with uncommon kindness, we will be pointing others to our Father in heaven. Are you up for it?

Lean into Him

> *"Look! I have been standing at the door, and I am constantly knocking. If anyone hears me calling him and opens the door, I will come in and fellowship with him and he with me."*
> (Revelation 3:20 TLB)

> *May we never tire of doing what is good and right before our Lord because in His season we shall bring in a great harvest if we can just persist. So seize any opportunity the Lord gives you to do good things and be a blessing to everyone, especially those within our faithful family.*
> (Galatians 6:9–10 VOICE)

This is how we've come to understand and experience love: Christ sacrificed his life for us. This is why we ought to live sacrificially for our fellow believers, and not just be out for ourselves. If you see some brother or sister in need and have the means to do something about it but turn a cold shoulder and do nothing, what happens to God's love? It disappears. And you made it disappear. (1 John 3:16–17 MSG)

Be kind and honest and you will live a long life; others will respect you and treat you fairly. (Proverbs 21:21 GNT)

Look into You

When you think of kindness, what thoughts or ideas does it conjure up in your mind?

Are you a kind person for the right reasons? Are your motives pure? What are some ways you can make sure your motivation for kindness remains (or becomes) sinless?

Who is the greatest example of kindness in your life? What did they do so well that made other people feel special?

What woman did you relate to the very most in this chapter? Why?

Jot down five women who need compassion right now. Come up with a few ways to show kindness to each of them. . .and then make it happen.

Live Uncommon

Lord, I know kindness matters to You. If not, it wouldn't have been listed as a fruit of Your Spirit. I want to be a woman who loves others well and shows them kindness instead of wrath. Help me become an agent of change so that my kindness is contagious. Help me show gentleness with pure motives so it's not misused. Help me treat myself with sympathy so I model that to the next generation. And help me share thoughtfulness freely rather than using it as a weapon or withholding it in anger. There's already too much of that in the world. I want to be uncommon, Father! In Jesus' name, amen.

CHAPTER 11

Uncommon Leadership

You may make your plans, but God directs your actions.
Proverbs 16:9 GNT

Deborah

If there was ever a powerful example of a woman from the Bible who was a strong leader, it was Deborah. What I deeply appreciate about her leadership style is that it wasn't shaped by the political climate or cultural norm of the day. Her vision for governance was shaped by her relationship with God. It's an uncommon way to lead because she listened for His voice, trusted His plan, and followed His lead.

At that time in history, women advisers were few and far between, but there were a few of them. Deborah was one. She was a charismatic leader, a respected prophetess, the only woman to hold a judicial position in Israel, and the wife to Leppidoth. Judges 4:4 gives us clear insight into the vital call God placed on her life. It reads, *"Israel's leader at that time, the one who was responsible for bringing the people back to God, was Deborah"* (TLB). She was the "it" girl, if you will. But even more, she wasn't concerned or distracted by what others thought about her position in a dominantly patriarchal society. Deborah knew without a doubt God had called her.

Israel was desperate for a strong leader. She was a struggling nation—spiritually starving, in civic disorder, and oppressed by enemies. Let's just say it was not her finest moment in history. So when God downloaded military instructions to Deborah, she passed them along to Barak. He was the military man God appointed to mobilize ten thousand men to fight King Jabin's mighty army led by Sisera. God even guaranteed a win for Barak at the Kishon River. It was in the bag. But Barak only agreed to the plan *if* Deborah promised to be there with him.

In verse 14 (TLB), she said to him, *"Now is the time for action! The Lord leads on! He has already delivered Sisera into your hand!"* At her command, Barak led his army and the battle was won. The Canaanites were defeated. His acceptance as commander, the ease of gathering troops, and Barak's immediate action at the Kishon River all point to her credibility as God's spokeswoman and her effective leadership.

Nobles followed her (Judges 5:13). Princes submitted to her authority (Judges 5:2, 15). And even warriors obeyed her command (Judges 4:6, 14–16). I'm grateful that God chose to include her story in the Bible because we need to see a strong woman modeled. The Lord values leadership because it empowers us to reveal the God-colors in the world. It enables us to add salt-seasoning, flavoring our corner of planet earth.

Sometimes we struggle to imagine we can lead at all. We buy into the lie that says we are *less than* men, weak and powerless. But Deborah's story proves that while society may tell us we are inferior. . .while we may struggle with our own insecurities. . .God sees uncommon leadership qualities within us. And if we say yes, He is faithful to bring them out.

There is a wrong way to lead, though. And sometimes we get it all messed up. When we lead without Jesus, our best efforts can often come out sideways. Deborah's success was rooted in her relationship with God. Good leaders— uncommon leaders—stay connected to His heart and move only when and how He directs.

Learning to be an effective leader is a sought-after topic. When I searched on Amazon for books that addressed leadership, I found over 136,000. With new titles coming in all the time, that number fluctuates day to day. The truth is, we want to know how to do it right. We want to be effective. We want to lead well—with good intentions and plans.

But sometimes our best-laid plans fail. The world is full of people whose good intentions come out in common ways—ways that turn us off, burn us out, and rile us up. Chances are you've seen these kinds of leaders at some point. Maybe you've been one of them. They're easy to spot because they leave quite an impression, and it's rarely a good one. As you think back, can you recognize any of these *common* leadership qualities in either yourself or others?

1) Failure to recognize the uniqueness of others
2) Lacks empathy and compassion
3) Makes it all about their own needs
4) Either overpowers when issues arise or is unwilling to confront them
5) Demanding in their requests
6) Operates from feelings of superiority, acts arrogantly, and lacks humility
7) Often overpromises and underdelivers
8) Lacks honesty and transparency
9) Is not trustworthy
10) Doesn't communicate with clarity

This is not an exhaustive list, but you get the picture. Bad leaders can make our lives miserable. They can sour our mood, ding our self-esteem, and make us spittin' mad. We lose trust, respect, excitement, and loyalty. And it results in relationships or situations becoming terribly dysfunctional. The problem is that too often, the world promotes and rewards leadership that divides rather than connects. It's the polar opposite of God's plan.

God has clear ideas of how He wants leaders to love and live. He wants us to be different in how we run our families, ministries, community groups, and companies. God wants us to lead in uncommon ways. And He inspired Paul to pen the details in Romans 12:9–13 (MSG): "*Love from the center of who you are; don't fake it. Run for dear life from evil; hold on for dear life to good. Be good friends who love deeply; practice playing second fiddle. Don't burn out; keep yourselves fueled and aflame. Be alert servants of the Master, cheerfully expectant. Don't quit in hard times; pray all the harder. Help needy Christians; be inventive in hospitality.*"

At first glance, it's clear to see how very different God's idea of leadership is compared to the one the world promotes. One fosters a sense of deep community, and the other does not. One has a strong moral foundation, and the other is worldly in nature. One is steeped in respect and love while the other is self-seeking. Based on the above verse from Romans—God wants us to lead in these uncommon ways:

1) *Be Authentic*

This means we have pure motives and are honest about our thoughts and ideas rather than trying to "pull one over" on others.

2) Steer Clear of Evil

This means we see the pitfalls and traps and avoid them at all costs. We make wise decisions and have discernment to see the dangers ahead.

3) Cling to Good

This means we make the hard choices, which are so often the right choices, too. We do what is right rather than do what is easy.

4) Love Deeply

This might be the most important characteristic for uncommon leaders. We need to deeply care for others, investing emotionally in their lives.

5) Put Others First

We realize it's not all about us, and we avoid making decisions solely based on what works for our lives and instead consider the impact on others, too.

6) Avoid Burnout

This means we take care of our emotional, spiritual, and physical selves so we're filled up and ready to pour into others.

7) Be Positive

This is a choice, because there are plenty of reasons to be negative. When life gets hard, when change comes without warning, when people disappoint. . .we have to decide to find the silver lining.

8) Stay the Course

An uncommon leader doesn't let anything get in the way of doing what God has asked. Instead of giving up, we continue to move forward and look for His open doors.

9) Pray with Intentionality

This means we bathe everything in prayer. We pray over projects, groups, individuals, situations, etc. We ask God's covering, wisdom, and heart in all we do.

10) Have a Servant's Heart

Too often, leaders' only concern is what's best for them, and they expect others to meet their needs. But God wants us to be more concerned with the needs of others.

God's economy always seems upside down, doesn't it? What the world touts as the best leadership blueprint is so often the exact opposite of the way God wants us to lead. His way is counterintuitive yet absolutely perfect. And when we choose to lead in His uncommon way, it will speak loudly into a world that's getting it all wrong. Let me introduce you to a woman who did just this.

Huldah

Huldah was a faith-filled prophetess living in Judah during a time when the nation was faithless. For over half a century, the kings didn't show respect to God or acknowledge His will for the nation, and eventually the people turned to pagan gods. But Josiah was now in power. He wanted to reestablish Yahweh as the one true God so Israel would turn back to Him.

Huldah's timing on the kingdom calendar was crucial because she had a reputation of being a truth teller. She didn't shy away from sharing hard truth either. Because she spoke whatever God asked her to share, everyone recognized Huldah as God's mouthpiece. Even King Josiah trusted her with very important issues. So when she courageously revealed God's judgment in 2 Kings 22. . .everyone listened and believed. Let me back up a bit.

Verse 8 (MSG) says, *"The high priest Hilkiah reported to Shaphan the royal secretary, 'I've just found the Book of GOD's Revelation, instructing us in GOD's ways. I found it in The Temple!'"* When they read its contents to the king, he freaked out and tore his clothes. He realized they had not been following the laws it contained. Remember, Josiah's deep desire as king was to realign the hearts of his people to God's, so this new information about undid him. I love what comes next.

Verse 14 tells us that Hilkiah (the priest), Ahikam (Shaphan's son), Achbor (Michaiah's son), Shaphan (the king's secretary), and Asaiah (the king's assistant) laced up their sandals and went to find Huldah. They wanted to get *her* interpretation. In Scot McKnight's book *The Blue Parakeet* he makes a powerful statement. "Huldah is not chosen because no men were available; she is chosen because she is truly exceptional among the prophets."[9] Her gender didn't matter. Her age didn't matter. She was an uncommon leader because she focused on what the Lord had to say rather than following the popular opinions of others.

The message she had for the young king was simple: God would bring death and destruction to the city and its people for their disobedience. It was inevitable and His anger unstoppable. But because Josiah was sorry and concerned, and because he humbled himself before God once he discovered the laws kept in the lost book, God's judgment on the nation would be postponed until *after* his death. Josiah's reign would be one of peace. And thirty-five years later, after the king had died, her prophecy came to pass.

Huldah not only *interpreted the document, but also confirmed its authenticity.* And because this lost book is generally considered to be the book of Deuteronomy, *it's scripture we're still reading today.* Huldah. . .you go, girl.

Sometimes as women leaders, we are mocked and criticized by men. Sometimes it's sexist, and other times it's societal. Even though God doesn't consider gender when He places a call on our life, humankind does. And the second-century rabbis weren't fans of Huldah or Deborah's leadership. In Dr. Claude Mariottini's article "The Rabbi's view on Huldah the Prophetess," he quotes Tal Ilan saying:

> *It should come as no surprise though that a later evaluation of Deborah's story does much to diminish her role. The rabbis, for example, take issue with her name—bee. They view it as a reflection of her negative character traits. They couple Deborah with the other prophetess— Huldah, whose name refers to an even more repulsive animal—a weasel. They say: "There were two arrogant women whose names were hateful. One was named 'wasp' and the other 'rat.' Of the wasp it is written: 'She sent and summoned Barak' (Judges 4:6) rather than go*

to him. Of the rat it is written: 'Tell the man'
(2 Kings 22:15) rather than 'tell the king' " (b.
Megillah 14b). Probably because in their time,
a woman in such a position was unthinkable,
even more than the biblical authors, the rabbis
were disturbed by women attaining such power
and they attributed them disagreeable personal
traits because they didn't like their success.[10]

Our leadership can sometimes be intimidating to others, which means we have to stand in confidence on the call God has placed on our life. Truth is, as Jesus followers we won't always make sense to the world. We weren't designed to fit in here. Instead, we were designed to shine Jesus into the world. Our job is to listen to what God wants us to do, even if it's not what the world thinks we should do.

It's called uncommon leadership. And it takes grit and courage. It takes constant prayer. It takes stamina and resolve. And when we ask God to equip us, He will. But even then, sometimes we get it all wrong.

Control versus Leadership

Early on in my marriage, I was the pants wearer. I was the self-proclaimed manager of the Scott family. It wasn't God-ordained; it was Carey-ordained. Because of the abuse I suffered as a child, it felt safer. And because of the home Wayne grew up in, allowing me to rule the roost felt familiar and palatable.

I had become an epic control freak with huge trust issues. It was how I protected myself from being hurt again. While it worked fairly well when I was single, it was becoming most unpopular in my marriage. And I knew unless I released the Herculean-strength grip I had on the reins, we'd end up in divorce.

I'll be honest—it wasn't easy to change. I liked being in control. I liked making the decisions. But I learned through some solid counseling that there's a big difference between control and leadership. Control is when we exercise our power over someone or something. We are forcing submission. But leadership is having the ability to guide and influence. It means we are ever aware of our capability and power but don't impose it inappropriately. Do you see the difference?

When I began giving up control, the weirdest thing happened. My husband began to step up and lead. Now I am not going to preach on the importance of letting husbands lead because Jesus already does that in multiple places in the Bible, including Ephesians 5:22. And there are so many good books on that topic available today. Even Deborah and Huldah had to find the perfect tension between being leaders in their community and giving their husbands respect within the confines of marriage.

Here is more truth to digest. God may ask you to lead in one place but not in another. Your job is to know the difference. For example, I take the lead on parenting because I am home more than Wayne. I am most often on the front lines when our kids have issues and struggles. And it gives me insight Wayne doesn't have, and because of that, he usually follows my lead.

In the same vein, I try not to take the lead on the bigger decisions for the entire family. I let my husband manage most of those. He sees the bigger picture with finances and long-term goals—both of which make me throw up in my mouth a little. Of course I have opinions and ideas—sometimes very strong—but being the leader of our family is what God has asked *him* to do. And if I stand in the way, we'll both be in disobedience.

And in each of our leadership roles within the family, we make sure we're leading God's way. We revisit the Romans 12 passage we unpacked earlier to make sure our leadership doesn't morph into control—that we don't move from uncommon leadership to the common kind.

Remember, good leaders always stay connected to the heart of God. They move only *when* and *how* God directs. Their identity is rooted in Jesus. They love deeply and lead with authenticity. They put others first because of their servant's heart. They stay the course, pray, and remain positive. They steer clear of evil and cling to good. And they take care of their own needs so they can avoid burnout.

Deborah and Huldah said yes to God in a time when women and leadership roles didn't mix. They said yes knowing they'd be fighting an uphill cultural battle. They didn't shy away from speaking hard truths, and God blessed them for it. Let's be women unafraid to say yes to God's plan for us to lead. Let's remember that leadership and control are not the same. And let's be forerunners who follow God's lead.

Lean into Him

> We should make plans—counting on God to direct us. (Proverbs 16:9 TLB)

*Don't let selfishness and prideful agendas take
over. Embrace true humility, and lift your heads
to extend love to others. Get beyond yourselves
and protecting your own interests; be sincere,
and secure your neighbors' interests first.*
(Philippians 2:3–4 VOICE)

*"And then you need to keep a sharp eye out for
competent men—men who fear God, men of
integrity, men who are incorruptible—and
appoint them as leaders over groups organized
by the thousand, by the hundred, by fifty, and by
ten."* (Exodus 18:21 MSG)

*I have a special concern for you church leaders.
I know what it's like to be a leader, in on
Christ's sufferings as well as the coming glory.
Here's my concern: that you care for God's flock
with all the diligence of a shepherd. Not because
you have to, but because you want to please God.
Not calculating what you can get out of it, but
acting spontaneously. Not bossily telling others
what to do, but tenderly showing them the way.*
(1 Peter 5:1–3 MSG)

Look into You

Where are the places God is asking you to step up
and lead in your family? Your community? Your career, etc.? Ask Him to show you what that looks like.

What was your biggest takeaway from our discussion on leadership versus control?

Looking at the list of ten ways to have uncommon leadership based on the Romans 12 passage, which one(s) might be the hardest to walk out? Why? How can you change that?

What impressed you the most about Deborah and/or Huldah? What life lesson(s) are you taking away from their story?

Think back to great leaders you've worked with, partnered with, lived with, or admired from afar. What did you like about being around them? What made it easy to follow them? Maybe find time to tell them face-to-face, send them a note, or e-mail them and say thanks for being a great example of an uncommon leader.

Live Uncommon

Lord, thank You for placing a call on my life to lead. It may be in my home, in my community, in my work, or in some other arena You choose. I want to be the kind of leader Paul mentioned in Romans 12 and am asking You to train me to lead with love and purpose. Help me remember the difference between control and leadership, and to always stay pure in my motives. Let Deborah and Huldah be positive reminders that women can lead well, even if it goes against the views of others. When You call people to lead, they have Your authority to do what You've placed before them. Give me the confidence to operate in that truth. Help me become an uncommon leader! In Jesus' name, amen.

CHAPTER 12

Uncommon Inheritance

I will open my mouth in parables; I will speak of ancient mysteries—things that we have heard about, things that we have known, things which our ancestors declared to us again and again. We will not keep these things secret from their children; rather, we will tell the coming generation all about the praise that is due to the Eternal One. We will tell them all about His strength, power, and wonders.
Psalm 78:2–4 VOICE

When I mention inheritance here, I'm not talking about the amount of money, the land, or any physical object you leave to those you love once you die. It's so much more important than that. The inheritance I'm unpacking in this chapter is deep and powerful, and our discussion is going to be very frank. Because this specific call to be uncommon affects others more than it affects you—or me. And because the stakes are high, we have to get this one right.

I've heard the story countless times, but it never gets old. And when my mom tells it, it usually brings tears to her eyes. She recounts several evenings during high school where she walked into her parents' room to let them know she was home, only to find her father kneeling next to the bed praying. She couldn't hear the words he spoke—they really didn't matter—but it was his faithfulness to commune with God that she inherited.

To this day, she keeps a physical prayer list by her blue

chair that keeps all her requests and petitions organized. My mom prays diligently and daily. She believes in the power of prayer and knows that God wants to hear the desires of her heart. For as long as I can remember, she has demonstrated the importance of connecting with God. I've inherited that from her.

While I had some serious wild-child days growing up and ran from God most of my life, my mom was diligent to pray and model a relationship with Jesus. When I'd mess up, she pointed me to God. When I failed, she pointed me to grace. When I wrestled with the desire to fight one more day in my brokenness, she spoke truth into my weary soul. My mom was persistent in keeping Jesus in the mix in my darkest days, and I'm certain she filled up countless prayer journals with just. . .*me*. And in my thirties, I fully stepped into that inheritance.

Looking back, I can now see where God was during those very hard times growing up. I better understand why He allowed a barrage of struggles to crash into my life, and I share that messy journey in grave detail in my book *Untangled*. There was purpose. There was divine training. It solidified my identity and gave me strength to step into the calling God placed on my life. And I know without a doubt that the rich spiritual inheritance my mother modeled has helped me embrace it and walk it out.

My kids are being trained up, too. My husband and I do our very best to show them that God is interested in all parts of their lives. They know He is not just a Sunday God or a crisis God. They are learning to recognize He is a God interested in every single silly or serious detail of their lives. We pray together. Do devotions together. Walk through

Bible studies together. And we share the places where we've seen God show up in our own lives.

My husband wrote personalized blessings for Sam and Sara when they were in elementary school. These blessings are anchored in scripture and filled with his hopes and dreams for each child—both now and in the future. They are rich with the spiritual inheritance we want for them. And almost every night as we gather as a family to pray before bed, he speaks these blessings out loud to the kids. It's a tradition we started and one we hope will ignite their hearts to continue in their own families someday.

Are we perfect in our pursuit to leave a rich spiritual legacy for our kids? Heck, no. I've screamed at them, shunned them in anger, spoken unloving things to their faces, let some unmentionable words slip out in anger, and had a million other mess-ups. Wayne has fumbled just as badly. But even in our imperfection, we are purposeful to deposit a beautiful inheritance in the hearts of our kids.

Here is some hard truth. I am praying this part of the discussion grabs your heart and opens your eyes because it's so very important to understand this. Take a deep breath. Ready? Each of us—you and me—*will* leave our kids (and those we have influence over) with some sort of spiritual inheritance. . .good, bad, or ugly. And we each get to choose which kind we pass on.

1) We can pass on *legalistic faith*, which crushes their spirit with unattainable rules and regulations.
2) We can pass on *guilt-induced faith*, which points out all the ways they're doing it wrong.

3) We can pass on *misguided faith*, where we teach incorrect theology based on something other than the Bible.

4) We can pass on *works-only faith* that reveals their need to earn salvation and acceptance by doing more and more and more.

5) We can pass on *enhanced faith* that says the Bible's teachings alone are not complete or enough.

6) We can pass on *weak faith* that declares God is not as powerful as He used to be, that He isn't interested in us as individuals, or that He is not in the miracle business anymore.

7) We can pass on *cultish faith*, where the church leader is the one worshipped rather than Jesus.

8) We can pass on *no faith* through atheism or agnosticism.

Or we can pass on an uncommon spiritual inheritance, where we show those we love what a relationship with Jesus looks like. . .stumbles, fumbles, and all. We can be real and authentic. We can walk out grace and forgiveness with honesty. We can talk about our struggles and where God is showing up. We can be transparent in the questions we have about being a Jesus follower. And we can model what trusting God no matter what looks like.

Maybe you recognize your own faith in the above list because it was passed on to you. And maybe you realize you're now passing it along to those you love. The truth is that the message of Jesus is simple, and it's never too late to embrace it. He will help us unlearn and unteach the wrong kind of faith if we ask.

Regardless of the inheritance you received from your parents, you can choose to leave a beautiful and rich spiritual inheritance for your family. That means every time you sow the Word into their hearts, every time you shine God-colors into their struggles, and every time you choose to live out your faith authentically, you will help set the tone for their relationship with Jesus. Yes, it is most certainly a *choice* to pass along an uncommon inheritance.

But here's where it gets tricky. Everyone has free will, meaning those you love will ultimately make their own decision about God. Their faith is not your ultimate responsibility, and thinking so is a lie from the Enemy. It's a trap that will leave you either beating yourself up or patting yourself on the back. Neither is good. You cannot force a spiritual inheritance on someone, but you can be intentional to create one. How?

- You can bring Jesus into your family in healthy ways.
- You can walk out your faith with integrity.
- And you can pray for God to invade the hearts of those you love.

So how are we going to do this well? Let's unpack Psalm 78:2–4 because it's a great starting place. It reads, *"**I will open my mouth** in parables; **I will speak** of ancient mysteries— things that we have heard about, things that we have known, things which our ancestors declared to us again and again. We will not keep these things secret from their children; rather, **we will tell** the coming generation all about the praise that is due to the Eternal One. **We will tell** them all about His strength, power, and wonders"* (VOICE, emphasis mine).

There sure is a lot of speaking and telling going on in this passage, isn't there? Go back and look at each bold instance to see exactly what they are sharing with others. I love this because it highlights the importance of using our *words* to pass on His goodness to the next generation. How else will they know it? Let's look at the three ways Psalm 78:2–4 says our words can help leave an uncommon inheritance.

1) We Share Testimonies

This means we share faith stories told to us and those we've experienced firsthand. We pass along encouragement from others because it reinforces our faith. Because the reality is that from time to time, we all need to be reminded that God is real, miracles still happen, and hope is worth holding on to.

And while some of us think faith should be kept quiet, this verse debunks it. We are told *not* to keep our mouths shut. . .and *not* to keep our testimonies from our kids. They need to hear of the power our heavenly Father had yesterday, has still today, and will have tomorrow. If you want to leave an uncommon inheritance, use the power of testimony to validate that God works in the lives of those who love Him.

2) We Give God Credit

When we hear stories about someone being healed from an incurable illness or experiencing restoration in a marriage destined for divorce, it strengthens us. When we watch an impossible situation work out, it encourages us. And when we give God credit for the hope and healing, it challenges others to get a bigger picture of who He is and what He can do.

To a believer, there is no luck. There is no chance. It

wasn't by accident. The planets didn't line up perfectly to create the desired outcome. And your horoscope had nothing to do with it. We have an all-powerful God who is in the details, always working things out for His glory and our benefit. It means whatever comes our way—hard or easy—we can trust He either brought it or allowed it for a divine purpose. It means we believe in God's hand versus pure coincidence. And if we want to leave an uncommon inheritance, we can start by pointing to God and giving Him the credit He deserves rather than hanging our hat on serendipity.

3) We Talk about His Awesomeness

Let's be women who understand the significance of revealing the strength, power, and wonders of God. Not only does it fill others with hope, it fills us, too. Think about it. Who would want to anchor their trust for a miracle in someone weak? Why would we risk our healing to someone inadequate? Why would we put our faith in an ineffective, feeble, spineless God? The truth is we wouldn't.

By nature, we are attracted to strong people. We want to date them, hang out with them, marry them, raise them. I always tell my kids, "I've never seen God with my own two eyes, but I've seen His power in my life more times than I can count." If we don't speak to the bigness of God, we will be shirking our responsibility to magnify Him. Our kids— and others we have the privilege to influence—need to know that He is a 24/7/365 can-do God. He has everything it takes to do whatever is needed. And while His answer to prayer is sometimes different than what we wanted, it doesn't change His ability or His authority or the fact that His heart for us is always good.

Something Wayne and I focus on in our family prayer time is telling God how awesome He is. It encourages our kids to see that Jesus is always the answer and worthy of our praise! It also helps us remember our position in relation to His. It feels natural to tell God, "Thank You for being in complete control" or "I know You are working everything in this situation for my good!" or even "You showed up so big in my messiness again. You are amazing!" It must delight God to know we trust and appreciate Him. . .and recognize His omnipotence. Make sure that part of the uncommon inheritance you leave is a deep knowledge of God's potency.

The Word gives us an amazing example of two women who were intentional to pass a rich spiritual inheritance on to Timothy—the young man who grew to become a leader in the early church.

Eunice and Lois

Timothy's mother and grandmother were credited in the sweetest way by Paul in 2 Timothy 1:5. It reads, *"What strikes me most is how natural and sincere your faith is. I am convinced that the same faith that dwelt in your grandmother, Lois, and your mother, Eunice, abides in you as well"* (VOICE).

Paul is recognizing that these two women had such deep confidence in Jesus—confidence in His power, His wisdom, and His goodness. And because they lived their faith so big—because they taught Timothy the teachings of Jesus—he became a pillar of the faith. He received the inheritance. Here is proof.

Second Timothy 3:15 (VOICE) says, *"Because since childhood you have known the holy Scriptures, which enable you to be wise and lead to salvation through faith in Jesus the Anointed."* He grew up with it. He knew scripture forward and backward. And here is why that's so remarkable.

In Eunice's day, scripture reading was reserved for men only. She may have heard scripture when it was read aloud, but she wouldn't have been able to sit with coffee in her favorite chair and read it like we can today. Actually, many women living in those times were illiterate, so even having access wouldn't have mattered. We don't know for sure, but Eunice may have taught Timothy from memory.

In addition, I imagine she and Lois shared their hard-won wisdom with him, guiding and correcting whenever the opportunity presented itself. They probably shared Bible stories about their forefathers in the faith. I'm sure he learned to pray by listening to their prayers and learned to live in faith by watching how they lived. And can you imagine the powerful testimonies Timothy had the privilege of hearing as he grew up? That, my friend, is spiritual inheritance on steroids.

Let's be women like that—women who pass along the right stuff to our kids and others. We don't want to hand down the wrong kind of faith because we know it can eventually cause them to walk away from God for good. Instead, we want to bless our kids with a deep understanding of God and prayer and living out faith every day.

Let's choose to give our kids the tools they need to thrive in their relationship with Christ rather than setting them up for failure, discouragement, and selfishness. Uncommon women aren't perfect, but they are purposeful to create a rich environment of faith to pass on to the next generation of believers. They are salt-seasoning, and their lives bring out the God-colors in the world. Let's be like that.

Lean into Him

We stand to inherit even more. As His heirs, we are predestined to play a key role in His unfolding purpose that is energizing everything to conform to His will. As a result, we—the first to place our hope in the Anointed One—will live in a way to bring Him glory and praise. (Ephesians 1:11–12 VOICE)

Love GOD, your God, with your whole heart: love him with all that's in you, love him with all you've got! Write these commandments that I've given you today on your hearts. Get them inside of you and then get them inside your children. Talk about them wherever you are, sitting at home or walking in the street; talk about them from the time you get up in the morning to when you fall into bed at night. Tie them on your hands and foreheads as a reminder; inscribe them on the doorposts of your homes and on your city gates. (Deuteronomy 6:5–9 MSG)

And he said to the people of Israel, "In the future, when your children ask you what these stones mean, you will tell them about the time when Israel crossed the Jordan on dry ground." (Joshua 4:21–22 GNT)

Let each generation tell its children what glorious things he does. (Psalm 145:4 TLB)

You are not to bow down and serve any image,
for I, the Eternal your God, am a jealous God.
As for those who are not loyal to Me, their chil-
dren will endure the consequences of their sins
for three or four generations. But for those who
love Me and keep My directives, their children
will experience My loyal love for a thousand
generations. (Exodus 20:5–6 VOICE)

Look into You

What kind of spiritual heritage was passed down to you?

How does hearing someone's testimony build up your faith? Who needs to hear yours?

Sometimes we are so quick to rationalize away healing or restoration or provision. How is it possible to give God the credit for every good thing?

Do you talk about God's awesomeness to others? What are three things you can do to be more intentional to praise Him to others?

What did you love the most about Eunice and Lois? How does their story inspire you to leave an uncommon inheritance?

Live Uncommon

Lord, I want to leave a rich spiritual inheritance for my kids and others I influence. Please help me remember to be intentional to share all the places You have shown up in my life. Remind me to give You credit for the ways You have blessed me and to be quick to help others see You in their circumstances, too. And I want to thank You for being such an awesome God! Help me remember that You are omnipotent and have the ability and authority to do whatever we need. Give me faith to hold on to that truth when it feels like You are far away and uninterested. And Father, help me be a Eunice to my children so they will grow up on fire for You! In Jesus' name, amen.

CHAPTER 13

Uncommon Love

Let love prevail in your life, words, and actions.
1 Corinthians 16:14 VOICE

*T*his just might be the hardest chapter for me to write. If you know anything about my past, you know that love has been tricky for me. Abuse marked me from a young age and messed up my understanding of what love was supposed to look like. It was the ground zero experience of my life in so many ways. Counselors have made that clear more than once. And while God has healed me of so much, looking back at how I fumbled through love and relationships is often sobering.

Love used to be a confusing emotion for me to navigate. I struggled to trust it. Too many times, people would say they loved me in one breath and then spew hateful words in the next. Friends would call me their bestie one day and then betray me the next. And I learned the hard way that some men would use the word *love* just to get what they wanted. The scripture above says love should prevail in words and actions, but for many of us that hasn't been our experience. Instead, love has been a journey of aches and pains.

I remember the moment I met Dean at the bar. Not the best place to meet a guy, but it was a reflection of where I was in my life at the time. He was so cute and had lots of muscles. He could two-step with the best of them, and this

Texas-born-and-raised girl fell for him fast. And soon—too soon—we declared our love to one another. But I quickly learned this wasn't love at all. It came with conditions and control.

It started with him trying to manage my time. When he couldn't get hold of me, he became paranoid. Dean began to obsess about spending all of our free time together and would get angry if I made other plans. He would say, "I just love you too much to share you." I'd be at the gym, and he would stand outside and stare at me through the window. I'd be at work, and he would run into my office and close the door behind him, trapping me inside so we could talk. And when I tried to call off the relationship, he told me no.

He professed his love with words, but his actions told me differently. The two didn't line up. To Dean, I was his property. Love didn't prevail; dysfunction did. The whole story is long and messy, but it was the catalyst for me to move to Colorado.

Within the first few months of being in Denver, I walked into a church again. It was a great experience, and I met some amazing friends. I jumped onto the leadership team of the singles' group, and God was connecting to my heart in a new way. And then I met Tom, my first husband. Friends, dysfunction always finds dysfunction. You can take that to the bank. I'm going to unpack this story more in chapter 18, so sit tight. The CliffsNotes version is that we divorced after just a few short years. My already broken heart was now shattered.

I decided that love was nothing special. It was common. It couldn't last. It wasn't safe. Because in most of my experiences, love did nothing but make me feel worthless. Love didn't prevail; it failed. And then I met my now-husband on an online dating service.

I wish you could meet Wayne. He is the most beautiful example of uncommon love. His love has helped heal some very tangled places in my heart. But when we first met, we were both pretty broken and beat up by life. Neither knew how to effectively receive and give love. But thanks to some darn good counseling and God's intervention, we just celebrated seventeen years of marriage.

He didn't always, but now he loves me like a pro. I hope he'd say the same about me. In our home and in our marriage, love absolutely prevails—in both our words and actions. And we're committed to passing that uncommon love on to our kids so it can be in their story, too. We want them to understand that not all love is created the same. That it takes intentionality to produce uncommon love. And that God is the key ingredient.

Here is a gold nugget just for you. This piece of knowledge may not seem profound, but many of us are fumbling through life and completely missing it. Ready? Okay. *When we choose to love others through **God's** strength instead of loving them through our **own** strength, love becomes uncommon.* You see, loving in our own human-sized strength is limited and conditional. But when we ask God to give us His strength so we can love someone who is challenging, our heart for them eventually changes. His love continues where ours ends.

But sometimes asking God to help us love better is tricky. There may be some people we don't want to love. When 1 Corinthians 16:14 tells us to *"Let love prevail in your life, words, and actions,"* we may shake our head or roll our eyes. It might bring up painful memories of our own experiences or convict us for how we've treated others.

Paul doesn't mince his words. He's clear in saying that in all situations and in all relationships, we need to love big. It must prevail. And we should let nothing get in love's way—not anger, bitterness, pride, justice, nothing. But to me, the key word in this verse is *let* because it indicates a decision needs to be made. We have to allow love to rule out. And once again, we are learning that to be uncommon is a choice.

It's easy to love those who are agreeable and kind. Even when they mess up, your love for them isn't shaken. They may annoy or frustrate you, but your love doesn't change. You might get spittin' mad when they make a bad choice or let you down, but no permanent damage is done. But you know what? God doesn't ask us to only love the easy ones. Nope. We're called to love *everyone*. And the Word is clear about it.

> *You have been taught to love your neighbor and hate your enemy. But I tell you this: love your enemies. Pray for those who torment you and persecute you—in so doing, you become children of your Father in heaven. He, after all, loves each of us—good and evil, kind and cruel. He causes the sun to rise and shine on evil and good alike. He causes the rain to water the fields of the righteous and the fields of the sinner. It is easy to love those who love you—even a tax collector can love those who love him. And it is easy to greet your friends—even outsiders do that! But you are called to something higher: "Be perfect, as your Father in heaven is perfect."* (Matthew 5:43–48 VOICE)

You and I are called to something higher. We're called to have uncommon love by showing compassion for those we consider unlovable and unforgivable.

Does this mean I have to muster up love for Dean and Tom? Do you have to love the husband who left you or the parent who created an unsafe home environment as you grew up? Do our kids have to love the bully at school who makes their life a living hell? Do we have to love the person who flipped us off on the highway or spread rumors about our family? *Well, yes.* And God will give you the strength to do so.

We can honor them with our words, choosing not to bad-mouth them. We can show integrity by not sharing the gory details of the situation. We can show decency by not retaliating out of our anger or hurt. This is the uncommon way, and it's something we can only do with God's help. Our words and actions preach either way. Let's remember that.

Listen, friend, if we're serious about being salt-seasoning and pointing out the God-colors in the world so others connect with the Lord, then we have to get this right. It's time to put on our big-girl pants. God is asking us to share uncommon love with the world. And we can't do that if we're filled with hate or anger or bitterness. We can't do that if we're still operating in an unhealthy understanding of what love is. *But we can do this.* It's a choice. And while it may not be easy, with God's strength it is doable.

Let's start by establishing three powerful truths:

1. We are *all* created in the image of God—
    you, me, and them. That means since He
    created us all in the same likeness, we're all
    worthy of being loved.

2. We are *all* sinful and capable of bad things. And it's Jesus' death on the cross that changed everything. Because He extended grace and forgiveness to everyone, we can, too. When we decide to let go of the offense, our heart is miraculously open to love those who have hurt us.

3. We *all* have the capacity to love. First John 4:19 tells us why, and it's because God first loved us. Simply put, His perfect love gives us the ability to love others.

Now that we know these truths, let's unpack six ways we can create and show uncommon love toward others in our lives.

1) Don't Rally the Troops

Nothing fuels anger and hate more than reliving the transgression over and over and over again with others. It may feel good when they take your side and pick up your offense, but it does nothing to soften your heart toward the one(s) God wants you to love.

2) Find Compassion for Their Story

You may never know what journey in life has caused people to become mean-spirited and conniving. You may never understand how they can be so ungrateful or demanding. But chances are their lives have been filled with pain and discouragement, and they're lashing out in their anger. You don't need to know all the details or receive an apology to extend grace. Be uncommon and just do it anyway.

3) *Invite the Holy Spirit*

As we discussed earlier, God never expected us to love in our own strength. Aren't you glad? Asking for God's Spirit to bring peace into your heart will help you find the compassion you're lacking. It will bring divine perspective when you want to inflict emotional pain. And even more, the Holy Spirit will activate your ability to see others through the eyes of Christ, because you will be reminded that He died on the cross for them, too.

4) *Create Healthy Boundaries*

Loving others doesn't mean you have to jump right back into a bad situation. Sometimes loving means developing healthy boundaries so you don't become too emotionally invested with a toxic person who has proven to be a serial offender. Keeping an appropriate distance keeps you from picking up another offense from the people you consider unhealthy.

5) *Balance Love and Truth*

Someone once told me that truth without love is brutality, and love without truth is hypocrisy. Isn't that spot-on? Finding the right balance can be like trying to walk over the Grand Canyon on a tightrope, in the snow, blindfolded. But if we want to have uncommon love, we will do our best to master it—maybe not perfectly, but purposefully.

Jesus always found the perfect tension between love and truth. And if we ever need His help to navigate the situation, asking for His help will assure we get it. Because if we leave out truth, we're setting others up for real trouble in the future, and if we leave out love, we will damage their self-esteem. Neither are good.

6) *Find Freedom in Forgiving*

Unforgiveness only keeps us tangled in the web of vengeful thoughts and ideas, and even worse hardens our heart. We won't be able to love the unlovable until we forgive the unforgivable. That is some meaty truth to chew on, friend. And honestly, when you choose to forgive someone, it's a love offering to yourself because it frees you from the power the situation or person has been holding over you.

Cultivating uncommon love for those who make it so hard is a choice that takes real guts and grit. It means we choose to love them through God's strength and not our own. It means we develop a divine perspective for others instead of an earthly one. And it means we choose to let love prevail in our lives, in our words, and in our actions. It won't be easy, but it will be worth it. Showing uncommon love is part of walking out Matthew 5:13–16 (remember our discussion from chapter 2?), because doing so will point others to Jesus.

One of my favorite quotes by C. S. Lewis is this: "Love is not affectionate feeling, but a steady wish for the loved person's ultimate good as far as it can be obtained."[11] He is saying that love is more than just a feeling. It's also a deep hope for goodness to surround every part of someone's life. And we see that kind of love in the story of Moses' mother.

Jochebed

Jochebed was a Hebrew slave living in Egypt and a God-fearing mom to Aaron, Miriam, and Moses. She was trying to raise kids during one of the darkest times in the history of her people. Pharaoh was on the war path. And it was his insecurity that put into motion an edict calling for the drowning of every Hebrew baby boy because he worried they may one day grow up to fight against him. In the middle of this mess, Moses was born. How might you have felt bringing new life into an atmosphere of death?

But here is where I deeply admire Jochebed. She wasn't afraid. Instead, she was filled with faith in God and love for her family. Hebrews 11:23 (VOICE) says, *"By faith Moses' parents hid him for three months after he was born because they saw that he was handsome; and they did not fear Pharaoh's directive that all male Hebrew children were to be slain."* Honestly, many of us might be freaking out thinking our son had a looming death sentence, but she chose to trust God.

This is significant because 1 John 4:18 says perfect love casts out fear. And maybe, just maybe, Jochebed was so aware of God that His perfect love took away her fear. That, in and of itself, is a perfect example of uncommon love.

At the end of three months, she knew it was no longer safe in her home. Exodus 2:3 (VOICE) says, *"When she could no longer keep him hidden away, she took a basket made of reeds, sealed it with tar and pitch, and placed her baby boy in it. Then she wedged the basket among the reeds along the edge of the Nile River."* As much as she loved her son and wanted to keep him tucked away with the family, she wanted him to have a chance at a full life even more. Can you imagine the uncommon love it took to send her three-month-old baby down the river with nothing more than hope?

As we discussed in the chapter "Uncommon Kindness," Pharaoh's daughter found him and adopted him as her own. During that time in Egypt, it was common for the upper echelon to have wet nurses for their kids. It helped them keep their figures and afforded them more sleep. And in a divine twist of events, Jochebed—whose true identity remained a secret—landed the job. It seems to me that God blessed her trust in Him and her uncommon love for Moses.

These three to four years gave her the perfect opportunity to instill the Hebrew culture into her son. She had the ability to introduce a basic knowledge of God, too. And I bet she took advantage of her time with Moses to speak value and worth into him. God graciously gave Jochebed time to lavish uncommon love on His anointed leader who would one day bring his very people out of slavery. What a beautiful story.

Let's not waste our time harboring bitterness and anger. Let's not hold on to unforgiveness and offenses. We are here to love the world through Jesus Christ, because only in His strength can we accomplish such a feat. We're called to love the unlovable and the easy alike. And if we ask God to tender our heart toward others, He will. He is the key to us being able to love others in uncommon ways.

Lean into Him

Anyone who does not love does not know God, because God is love. (1 John 4:8 VOICE)

So, chosen by God for this new life of love, dress in the wardrobe God picked out for you: compassion, kindness, humility, quiet strength, discipline. Be even-tempered, content with

*second place, quick to forgive an offense. Forgive
as quickly and completely as the Master forgave
you. And regardless of what else you put on,
wear love. It's your basic, all-purpose garment.
Never be without it.* (Colossians 3:12–14 MSG)

*My loved ones, let us devote ourselves to loving
one another. Love comes straight from God, and
everyone who loves is born of God and truly
knows God.* (1 John 4:7 VOICE)

*"Do not take revenge on others or continue to
hate them, but love your neighbors as you love
yourself. I am the LORD."* (Leviticus 19:18 GNT)

*If anyone boasts, "I love God," and goes right on
hating his brother or sister, thinking nothing of
it, he is a liar. If he won't love the person he can
see, how can he love the God he can't see? The
command we have from Christ is blunt: Loving
God includes loving people. You've got to love
both.* (1 John 4:20–21 MSG)

Look into You

What has love looked like in your life? How was it
modeled growing up, and what has your experience
been?

Does love prevail in your words and actions? If not,
in what ways can you change that?

We are called to love everyone—even the unlovable. Who do you need to ask God for help to love? What is He saying to you about it right now?

Look back at the six ways we can create and show uncommon love. Which ones are the most challenging for you and why? What is your plan now?

What did you love the most about Jochebed's story?

Live Uncommon

Lord, it's so easy to have compassion for kind and caring people, but it's a whole other story to love those who are unlovable. Please forgive me for being selective, because that's not Your plan for us. I want to have love for everyone, but I need Your help to tender my heart. I need Your strength to love the ones who are challenging. Because more than anything, I want to get this right. Thank You for Jochebed's example. Help love prevail in my life just like hers. In Jesus' name, amen.

CHAPTER 14

Uncommon Obedience

"So why do you call me 'Lord' when you won't obey me?"
Luke 6:46 TLB

I sat up in bed and gasped. *What in the world was that?*
Just moments earlier, a divinely inspired PowerPoint presentation finished playing in my mind. The vision was of me speaking in all types of settings—in homes, at churches, and even in big arena-type venues. In it, I spoke about my life experiences, quoted Bible verses, and unpacked biblical stories. Each snapshot lasted only a few moments, but the vision lasted for what seemed like an hour. And when it was over, I freaked out. At that time in my life, I was actively running the other direction from God.

"No way, God. I am not interested. You haven't been there for me, so I won't be there for You either." In a huff, I rolled over and tried to sleep, but my mind was racing. What was God thinking? With my background and current season of sinning, why would He want someone like me to step onto the front lines in ministry? And with all the evil He had allowed into my life, why would I even consider it? I tossed and turned in frustration as I tried to understand what God had just showed me. But deep down, there was a twinge of excitement stirring in my spirit.

Saying yes to God isn't easy because it requires some-thing from us. We may have to give up time or sin, comfort or security, resources or control, and other things we hold dear. It's costly, too. We may have to tell our story on stage or in a book. God might ask us to share the Gospel with people in another country. Obeying God is a choice.

When we say yes to Him no matter the cost, it becomes uncommon obedience. It means we trust God more than we worry about the details. It means we believe God knows what He is doing. And even more, having uncommon obedience means we know there is a promise on the other side.

Colossians 3:23–24 reads, *"Whatever you do, work at it with all your heart, as though you were working for the Lord and not for people. Remember that the Lord will* **give you as a reward** *what he has kept for his people. For Christ is the real Master you serve"* (GNT, emphasis mine). So what is the promise here? A reward.

This verse tells us that when we obey, there is an eternal reward we'll receive from God for doing what He asked. I don't know about you, but this truth settles my sometimes-rebellious heart that wants to do things my own way. It makes the risk of saying yes worth it. It's a sweet reminder that God sees our *yes* to Him. . .and honors it.

Maybe you think our motive for obeying shouldn't only be because we want the blessing. I hear you. But think about it. Every time we obey, it's because there's a hope attached to it. We're faithful in marriage because we want it to succeed. We follow traffic laws to stay ticket- and accident-free so our insurance rates don't increase. We raise kids in a godly home in the hope they'll develop their own personal relationship with Jesus as adults. In that same vein, obeying God because we know there's a blessing when we do isn't selfish. It's motivation. And even more, it breeds uncommon obedience.

The next morning after the vision, I sat with my Bible open waiting for God to speak to me about the night before. Scripture after scripture confirmed His faithfulness and trustworthiness. "God, if this is something You are asking me to do, You will have to open the doors. I'm too scared to fail and embarrass myself. If You bring opportunities to me, I will say yes." Two weeks later—out of the blue—the MOPS (Mothers of Preschoolers) coordinator at church asked me to share the story of how God restored my marriage. And with my knees knocking and pits sweating, I stood up and shared my story.

Even today—twelve years later—God is still bringing ministry opportunities my way. I've experienced Hebrews 10:36 where He promises to bless obedience. And while my heart is burdened to speak truth into the hearts of women, I'm still motivated knowing He will continue to reward the time and effort I've poured in. I will receive the promise.

Here is some powerful truth I want to put in your lap. Grab your highlighter. Here we go. *The Enemy likes to intimidate us by making what God is asking look too big and too hard.* When God gave me the vision of speaking on stages, it freaked me out. At that time, I was rarely cracking open my Bible. I couldn't imagine how I would get from where I was. . . to where He wanted me to be. And so we say no to God. That's a common response.

But having uncommon obedience means we see right through that demonic scheme. Instead of worrying about the big picture, we focus only on the next step God wants us to take. We don't get weighed down by the *how*. . .we just say yes to the *now*.

For me, it was agreeing to speak at MOPS. That was the next step God revealed. Don't be overwhelmed with the end result. Instead, choose to say yes to every next step.

So what is God asking you to do next? Maybe it's choosing to forgive. Maybe it's agreeing to be on the committee. It could be putting pen to paper or joining the health club. Maybe it is making a better choice each time that addiction calls out to you. It might be a volunteer opportunity, a softening toward your husband, more involvement with your kids, or standing up for what's right. Uncommon obedience is choosing to take the *next step.* Just like you delight in your children, or team members or employees, when they do what you've asked, our Father in heaven delights, too. He created us with a purpose. We have a kingdom-focused assignment we may never fully realize this side of heaven. So when we obey and say yes, we are one step closer to fulfilling God's plan for our life.

Here's where it gets tricky—at least for me. So often, obedience takes grit because it requires us to step out of our comfort zone. It's an exercise in uncomfortableness. It stretches our limits. It pulls us out of contentment and security. And it can be unnerving. Obedience often makes us face our insecurities because we lack confidence in our skills and abilities. But here is some amazing news that will allow you to breathe. Ready? *God doesn't call the equipped. He equips the called.*

Let me give you an example. God called me—an introvert who struggles with shame and unworthiness—to stand on stage and share my journey. He has asked me—a woman so knotted up in deep insecurity—to unpack her story with the world. And even today, God asks me to walk out hard ministry when there are times I'd rather walk away.

When we have uncommon obedience, we're constantly

called out of our comfort zone. And in response to our *yes*, God constantly blesses us for it. So it shouldn't surprise you that the Enemy is constantly finding ways to discourage us from taking that next step.

Here are the three most common ways the Enemy dissuades us:

1) We Run or Hide

We try to hide from His view. We avoid faith-filled community. We plug our ears and say, "Na-na-na," trying to drown out God's voice. We decide we can't be responsible for things we didn't hear. . .right? Somehow the Enemy has convinced us that God's plan is restricting. That His will for our life will be a drag. Or even that what He wants us to do is silly or too risky. And so we run and hide.

Think of all the Bible characters who tried to run or hide from God—Adam and Eve, Moses, Jonah, Elijah, to name a few. They eventually connected with God, and their lives were anything but boring. They had adventure and drama. . . ups and downs. . .victory and failure. But in the end, they played a vital part in history. He is inviting us to do the same.

God is in relentless pursuit of our heart and healing, because His plan for us is full of hope and expectation. You know what's scary? If we stay unavailable, we could use up our one and only life on nothing significant. It's our choice. If we want to live uncommon and point others to Jesus, we have to embrace our calling rather than run from it.

2) We Excuse Ourselves

The Enemy is in the shame-making business, and we are his target customer. If we buy into the lie that says who we are is not good, we'll end up excusing ourselves from serving God. We will decide our shady past makes us ineligible or our current season of sinning disqualifies us. But God has a history of using common people to do uncommon things.

Abraham was old, and Sarah laughed when she heard God's promise for her life. Moses stuttered, had anger issues, and killed a man. David was a murderer and had an affair. Jacob was a liar, and John was self-righteous. Saul (before he was Paul) murdered countless Christians. Jeremiah battled depression and suicidal tendencies. Noah was a drunk and Rahab a prostitute. Now if God can use this motley crew, He can use you and me. Nothing we've done, are doing, or will do bans us from doing kingdom work. Don't let anything keep you from stepping out in obedience to God.

3) We Question the Call

Sometimes it's hard to know if the voice we're hearing is God's. It can be confusing because we are always processing so much information. The world's voice is loud. Our voice is biased. The Enemy's voice is deceiving. And God's voice can be challenging. So instead of pressing in, we shut down.

We should be discerning in whose voice we choose to obey. That is wise. So let's do what we can to confirm rather than sitting paralyzed in confusion. The Bible is our blueprint for living, which means we can use it to authenticate what messages are from God and which ones are not. If what He is asking aligns with His character and the Word supports it, chances are it is divine. And even better, if we take a step in faith and get it wrong, God will course correct in love.

Let's meet someone who not only knew God's voice but obeyed without question.

Hagar

Her story unfolds in chapters 16 and 21 in the book of Genesis, and you can't help but connect with her story in one way or another. Hagar was an Egyptian who left her homeland to become a slave to Abram and Sarai. She was a trustworthy helper in the household, and that led to being promoted to one of Sarai's maidservants—an important position to hold. Sarai probably had a measured affection for Hagar because she was about to trust her with something huge.

In desperation to continue the family line, she told her husband to sleep with Hagar. And because Sarai was struggling to get pregnant, Hagar was expected to be a surrogate so the couple could build their family through her. And as a maidservant, she had no voice in the matter. Abram agreed to the plan, and Hagar became pregnant.

Soon afterward, scripture says she began to despise her mistress. Rather than take responsibility for forcing the connection, Sarai blamed Abram for Hagar's cruelty. And rather than manning up and handling the situation, Abram told Sarai to figure it out. She was mean-spirited right back to Hagar—and the pregnant maidservant ran away. Sounds like a plot on Jerry Springer, doesn't it?

Here is where uncommon obedience came into play. An angel appeared to Hagar, promised a long line of descendants, gave her the name to call her soon-to-be-born son, and then gave her a hard command in Genesis 16:9 (VOICE): *"Hagar, go back to your mistress, and change your attitude. Be respectful, and listen to her instructions. You're pregnant, and you need to go home."* And she obeyed.

She could have kept running, ignoring the angel's command. She could have justified it in her mind, deciding it was safer for her and the baby to leave for good. But because she saw the bigger picture and chose to trust God's promise, she turned around and went home. She exhibited uncommon obedience.

The story complicates again in Genesis 21 with jealousy between Sarai and Hagar. I want to encourage you to read the rest of their story; it's a good one. But the part of her life I want you to take away is her submission to God. While she may have pushed boundaries and rebelled against rules with the family, she didn't mess around with what God asked of her. She was quick to obey and was greatly blessed because of it. Her son Ishmael became the father of a great nation.

The Widow of Zarephath

God directed Elijah to pack his bags and head to Zarephath, assuring him that He would provide food through a widow. So Elijah obeyed and left at once. He arrived in town to find the widow picking up sticks by the city gate. Widows were considered second-class citizens in that day and were often left to fend for themselves and their children, so we can assume she was probably poor and desperate.

He called out, asking her to bring him water. As she was getting it for him, he also asked for a piece of bread. While he didn't know it, he was literally asking her to give him everything she owned. Her response in 1 Kings 17:12 (VOICE) reveals her state of heart and mind:

> *As certain as the Eternal One, your True God lives,*
> *I don't have any bread. In fact, I am starving. I*
> *don't have anything except for a bit of flour in a*

bowl and a few drops of oil in a jar. I was gathering
sticks when you arrived to make a fire so that my son
and I could eat one last bite of food and then die. It's
all over for us.

What a heartbreaking situation. But then Elijah promises a
blessing for her obedience.

Elijah told the widow to make food for him and then
make food for her and her son with what was left. He said
God promised that her flour and oil would not run out
before He sent rain to end the drought. What a crossroads.
Would she go into self-preservation mode and refuse to
obey, or would she trust this word from God? The widow
chose to feed the hungry prophet with her last bit of food.
Can you imagine what kind of uncommon obedience it
would take to meet a stranger's needs over your own? God
stirred her heart, and she followed His prompting. And the
divine payoff was more than she could have ever imagined.

It's so gracious of God to include stories like these in
the Bible because they offer us proof He will honor our
yes. We need to know God will bless our obedience every
time we say yes. We need to know He sees it and rewards
us for doing the hard thing. Just as Hagar had to return to
a hostile environment and the widow had to give away her
last meal before they received the blessing, we, too, have to
choose to take the first step and trust God, knowing we will
be rewarded. Uncommon obedience is a choice based on a
promise.

If we want to live differently than the world so others
see Him, then being willing to do what God asks of us is

vital. It's common to obey in the easy. But it's uncommon to obey in the hard. And the good news is that God will bless both.

Lean into Him

I have decided to take the path of faith; I have focused my eyes on Your regulations.
(Psalm 119:30 VOICE)

Without delay I hurry to obey your commands.
(Psalm 119:60 GNT)

"Do what the LORD says is right and good, and all will go well with you. You will be able to take possession of the fertile land that the LORD promised your ancestors." (Deuteronomy 6:18 GNT)

"If you live by my decrees and obediently keep my commandments, I will send the rains in their seasons, the ground will yield its crops and the trees of the field their fruit. You will thresh until the grape harvest and the grape harvest will continue until planting time; you'll have more than enough to eat and will live safe and secure in your land." (Leviticus 26:3–5 MSG)

"Now get yourselves ready. I'm sending my Angel ahead of you to guard you in your travels, to lead you to the place that I've prepared. Pay close attention to him. Obey him. Don't go against him. He won't put up with your rebellions

because he's acting on my authority. But if you obey him and do everything I tell you, I'll be an enemy to your enemies, I'll fight those who fight you." (Exodus 23:20–22 MSG)

Look into You

Obedience is tricky because it gets a bad rap. Before reading this chapter, what were your thoughts on it? How have they changed after reading it?

Scripture is clear that God blesses our obedience. How does this make you feel?

Where is God asking you to obey? What has kept you from it? What will happen if you don't?

We discussed three common responses we can have when God is asking for our obedience. Can you see yourself in any of them, and how will you respond differently now?

Hagar and the widow gave us beautiful examples of obeying in the hard. What was your biggest takeaway?

What do you need to change so you can have uncommon obedience?

Live Uncommon

Lord, sometimes I struggle to obey You. Forgive my rebellion and those times I try to run and hide. I get scared and overwhelmed, and I stop trusting that You will bless my *yes*. I forget that You don't call the equipped. You equip the called. I needed to know that! And thanks for including stories like Hagar and the widow because they remind me that You will do what You say You'll do. Even more, I appreciate that scripture is full of reminders that You reward those who obey Your commands. I want to be one of those kinds of women! Please give me the courage to have uncommon obedience. In Jesus' name, amen.

CHAPTER 15

Uncommon Perseverance

Simply endure, for when you have done as
God requires of you, you will receive the promise.
Hebrews 10:36 VOICE

I recently had a crisis of calling. It wasn't the same as a
crisis of faith, because I am a Jesus-girl through and through.
God has pulled me from the pit so many times I no longer
doubt He is who He says He is. I know He's alive and active
and loves me deeply. So I wasn't questioning my belief in
God. I was questioning belief in the call on my life—because
sweet mother, doing what God asks can be hard, and it requires so much from you. Faith is not a passive sport.

As I write this, I'm in the middle of a year full of
heart-thumping disappointments—the kind where you
shake your head and say, *What just happened?* I'm no stranger
to being let down by people. It's just part of life. . .right?
And I know the value of putting on your big-girl pants and
walking through hard circumstances. Life can be more challenging than we bargained for. This is the reality we all face,
we all navigate, and hopefully, we all learn from.

But every once in a while, something or someone pierces
those deeper places in your heart, and it's hard to reconcile.
You just didn't see it coming. Life was going along just fine
until it wasn't, and you're left gasping at the truth of what
just happened because it seems so impossible. And rather
than rise up and fight. . .instead of strapping on the armor of

God and stepping onto the battlefield. . .you want to quit.

That's where I've been over the past six months. Finding my footing and catching my breath in this season has been one of the hardest things I have ever done. Because it wasn't just one thing—it was several painful events that collided. I've watched a dream die, a friendship crumble, and someone prosper greatly off of my work. Being overwhelmed by grief, I have tried to hold on to hope with everything in me, but my heart has been weary.

Maybe you are here, too. Chances are life in your corner of the world is big and hard and discouraging, and you are gasping for air as well. There doesn't seem to be a lack of curveballs these days. Hurtful words, painful breakups, scary diagnoses, empty bank accounts, mind-numbing injustices, oppressive relationships, and unmet needs knock us down. Maybe most of the time you get right back up. You're a strong woman with the power of Jesus behind you, and rather than give up, you get back on the battlefield. That's usually me, too. But every once in a while, the situation feels heavier and we can't find our footing. And we question God—*Where are You? Why did You allow this? Why didn't You save me? Why aren't You fixing it?*

Those are fair questions to ask. God can handle every one of them, and He loves authentic conversations full of raw honesty. He knows life is hard. And because God loves us so much, He invites you and me to ask Him anything at any time. We can go right to our heavenly Father and drop all the questions we want at His heavenly feet. God knows that if we are asking, it means we are engaged. This is uncommon perseverance because it has an eternal perspective. The last thing He wants is for us to give up because there's a promised blessing on the other side of obedience. We unpacked it in great detail in the last chapter and learned that truth is confirmed by Hebrews 10:36.

Here is the problem. Too many of us are giving up the fight because the battle is long and messy. Rather than digging in our heels and refusing to quit, we give in because it just feels better. But friend, this is where the rubber meets the road. This is where we find out if we're just playing faith or if we believe God is who He says He is. This is where we have the opportunity to walk in uncommon perseverance.

Think back to a time when your situation felt out of control but you hung in there until the very end. You fought hard, and it took everything in you. Even though you were bloodied and bruised, you made it across the finish line. Can you connect a blessing to that perseverance? Maybe your marriage was restored. Maybe your prodigal came home. Maybe your finances turned around. Maybe your heart is peaceful. Maybe you gained understanding or grace. Friend, how was your perseverance recognized?

Now think back to a time when you gave up rather than endured. Oh I have many to pick from. I don't know about you, but I've spent most of my life giving up and giving in. I lacked the confidence and courage to stay the course. Here are some of the ways we justify quitting.

1) *It's Too Hard*

We can be such cupcakes, can't we? When we join a Bible study and it gets intense or too personal, we stop going. When we try something new and don't succeed immediately, we complain and quit. When the path to healing is muddy, rocky, and uphill, we turn back around for smoother roads.

And we justify it by saying *life is too short* or *maybe it wasn't meant to be* or *life is already hard enough.*

Here's where this mind-set backfires big-time. Our kids (and others we influence) follow our lead. They watch us give up and follow suit. Sometimes rather than empower, we rescue them or fix it. They don't have to persevere; they just have to whine to mommy. And other times, we give them permission to quit because what happened wasn't *fair.* Even worse, we tell them they *deserve* to be happy. What are we doing?

Let's remember that God will either give us the uncommon perseverance we need to walk through trying situations or He will point us in another direction. Prayer and time in His Word will help us know which one it is. We were not created to be quitters.

2) I'm Not Strong Enough

Honestly, sometimes I don't think I am—especially when I'm already so weary in the battle. At the core, *I'm not strong enough* is often the cover phrase for *I don't think I have what it takes so I'm quitting.* But when we use this excuse, we're forgetting one very important thing. With Jesus, we can do all things. It's not about our strength; it's about His. And even more, there's a hard-won satisfaction that comes from pressing through to the end. There's a personal satisfaction and a divine promise of blessing on the other side. That means we can know with certainty that our uncommon perseverance won't be in vain.

3) It Requires Too Much of Me

This justifies walking away. And it can almost look selfless because we've decided there are other things—more important things—that need our time and attention. Maybe we think our family is too needy and our job too busy, our marriage too heavy, our health too shaky, or our finances too scary. So instead of being tenacious, we quit. We forget that if God asks us to persevere through something, we can trust He has a complete picture of the demands on our time.

Let's look at how women in Bible times walked in uncommon perseverance.

Noah's Wife

Chances are we grew up hearing the story of Noah and the ark. We learned how God used it to judge the world. We probably sang songs in preschool or Sunday school about how the animals went into the boat two by two. We may have even had an ark mobile that hung over our baby crib. This is one of the most beloved stories in the Bible.

Genesis 6–9 tells the story of Noah, with the majority of the focus being on him—a man who lived in a way that God considered righteous. But his wife is never mentioned. Interesting, huh? Now we know that 98 percent of the time, behind every good man is a good woman. So maybe since we don't have proof through scripture, we can give her the benefit of the doubt. And because we know the ark took 120 years to build—years full of ridicule from their community—it would make sense to assume she had uncommon perseverance to stand by her man.

During the building, she probably had to give up date night with Noah. Perhaps she had to shoulder more responsibility around the house, which included raising children. Many women would have walked out of that kind of a marriage, thinking they deserved more. And watching your husband's reputation go down the toilet might make some women run for the hills so they wouldn't be labeled the same. But not this woman. She weathered it all, and God blessed her for it. She offers a beautiful example of uncommon perseverance.

Rizpah

Rizpah was one of Saul's concubines. When the Gibeonite leaders told David they wanted seven of Saul's descendants so they could kill them in retribution for what Saul tried to do to them, he agreed. You can read the entire story in 2 Samuel 21.

Armoni and Mephibosheth were among the seven, and after their death the bodies were left on the mountain where the execution took place. Verse 10 (VOICE) tells us that Rizpah *"spread out sackcloth on a rock to make a place to sit; and from the time her sons died until the rain fell in late autumn, she refused to let the birds or wild animals desecrate the bodies."* This vigil was her last act as their mother, and it lasted for months. Her uncommon perseverance honored her sons in their dishonorable death.

Consider how much this required of her. She left comfortable living arrangements to take up residence on a mat spread over rocks. Imagine the smell of rot under a hot sun. Imagine the sight of watching your children's bodies decay. Think about the time she had to ruminate over the good memories and the hard memories. I cannot imagine her grief. Even when most of us would have packed up and returned home, she remained until the weather conditions told her it was time to leave. Rizpah did the hard thing. Her endurance reminds us we can, too.

The Syro-Phoenician Woman

Matthew 15 introduces us to a Canaanite woman whose daughter was possessed by a demon. She was desperate for help and knew Jesus was able to heal. When she saw Him, she cried out for His help, but Jesus said nothing in response. Scripture says she continued to wail—so much so that the disciples asked Him to do something to shut her up. They were annoyed. Men may not understand our desperation as moms, but Jesus most certainly does. And He honors our uncommon perseverance.

In verse 25, we're told she knelt before Christ and begged, *"Lord, help me!"* Will you put yourself in her sandals for a moment and imagine the distress and determination she must have been feeling? She had probably tried everything she knew to heal her daughter and was battling hopelessness. And then Jesus responds, *"Woman, you have great faith. And your request is done"* (v. 28 VOICE). Immediately, the demon fled her daughter's body. She was healed right then and there. This mom's persistence paid off.

Here's the bonus to that story. Think of the testimony she had to share with those around her. They knew of the demonic possession and watched a mom's perseverance pay off. Seeing her steadfastness rewarded undoubtedly left a mark in their own memory—one that could make the difference between giving up and pushing through in their own tough situations. This woman's resolve had the ability to make ripple effects in her immediate community and possibly even for generations to come.

Having uncommon perseverance doesn't mean hard seasons won't cause us to question *where* God is and *why* He is allowing it. Life storms may shake the foundation of our faith, and we may need God to remind us He is in control. We might crave His peace to steady us in the midst. We may need spiritual eyes and ears to find Him in it. And it may take everything we have to hold on to the truth that God is good and His ways are right, but we have to muster the courage to persevere through our storms because blessing is on the other side.

Here is a nugget of truth that will offer perspective when we need it the most. Ready? *Every one of your struggles, all of your pain, and every moment of your suffering has a divine purpose.* God uses it all. When He asks us to stand strong and endure, He uses every ounce of the process for our benefit and His glory. He uses it to strengthen our faith. . .build our trust. . .heal our hearts. . .open our eyes. . .empower our calling. . .and direct our path. And when we try to shortcut the journey, we'll miss out on lessons and blessings along the way. Even more, when we get to the end of our rope. . .God is there. He is the one who takes ordinary perseverance and supersizes it. God is why uncommon perseverance is possible.

I don't know about you, but I need to know this. I need to know God will meet me as I persevere through the hard times. I need to know God will give me strength. And while I may not understand why the life storms come my way, I trust there is good reason. I choose to trust God—at least most of the time I do.

James 5:11 offers us a beautiful snapshot of why perseverance matters. *"What a gift life is to those who stay the course! You've heard, of course, of Job's staying power, and you know how God brought it all together for him at the end. That's because God cares, cares right down to the last detail"* (MSG).

Job's redemption is one of the most amazing stories from the Bible. You can read the entire account of his life in his self-titled book. He is the poster child for James 5:11. Although he was considered upright and blameless, he experienced epic loss in every area of his life—his children, his material possessions, his health. His living nightmare lasted for nine months, yet he remained steadfast in his love and trust of God. And in the end, Job was rewarded with a double portion of everything he lost.

God honored Job's resolve to believe He was good, even when it looked as if God had abandoned him. Job is yet another example of what uncommon perseverance looks like.

I'm challenging you to be a woman who lives differently than how the world tells you to live. Be a woman who always carries hope in her heart. I know there are plenty of excuses and reasons for throwing in the towel when life gets hard, but please don't. We need to demonstrate to others the value of staying power. They need to see a sweet victory that comes from fighting through to the very end. Let's be women to model uncommon perseverance.

So if you're in a dark season trying to make sense of your situation. . .if God is asking you to walk through a very difficult circumstance. . .if you are about to give up or give in. . .hold on.

Hold on to the truth that God is good.

Hold on to the certainty that His heart is *for* you.

Hold on to the reality that He won't leave you stuck.

Hold on to the fact that there's a divine purpose in what you are walking through.

And never forget that your uncommon perseverance comes with a promise of blessing.

Lean into Him

May we never tire of doing what is good and right before our Lord because in His season we shall bring in a great harvest if we can just persist. (Galatians 6:9 VOICE)

But you, friends, must not become tired of doing good. (2 Thessalonians 3:13 GNT)

I am convinced and confident of this very thing, that He who has begun a good work in you will [continue to] perfect and complete it until the day of Christ Jesus [the time of His return]. (Philippians 1:6 AMP)

So let's do it—full of belief, confident that we're presentable inside and out. Let's keep a firm grip on the promises that keep us going. He always keeps his word. Let's see how inventive we can be in encouraging love and helping out, not avoiding worshiping together as some do but spurring each other on, especially as we see the big Day approaching. (Hebrews 10:22–25 MSG)

Look into You

We all go through life storms that feel so big and overwhelming that we want to give up. How have you responded to these storms in the past? And how will you respond to the next one that comes your way?

We talked about the three ways we justify quitting rather than persevering. Which one(s) could you identify with and how?

Scripture is clear that if we endure there is a blessing on the other side. Can you think of a time when you saw this play out in your life or someone else's?

We looked at three women who offered a beautiful picture of uncommon perseverance. Which one connected with you the most and why?

What does having uncommon perseverance look like to you?

Live Uncommon

Lord, sometimes giving up seems like the best option because what's ahead feels like too much. But I know You bless me when I stand strong. Thank You that something sweet is on the other side of persevering. It helps knowing my hard work will be rewarded, especially since it's going to take so much of me to walk out. Thank You for not asking me to endure in my own strength but instead making Your strength and resolve available to me if I ask. And I am asking right now. I need Your help to get through this tough season. Please give me the courage and motivation to keep pressing forward. I love You. In Jesus' name, amen.

CHAPTER 16

Uncommon Prayer

Don't be weary in prayer; keep at it; watch for God's answers,
and remember to be thankful when they come.
Colossians 4:2 TLB

*I*n the 2016 movie *War Room*, we are introduced to Miss
Clara, a woman who understands what uncommon prayer
looks like. When life got tough, she got down on her knees.
She didn't waste time complaining. She didn't give up because the battle was too hard or too long. She didn't settle
into feelings of hopelessness. Instead of responding to tough
situations in her flesh, she took them right to the Lord. Miss
Clara stormed the gates of heaven with petitions and prayers
and watched as God intervened. What a beautiful example
of faith. I want to be just like her when I grow up. Amen?

Prayer can be tricky to fully understand, though. There
is mystery to it that can't be explained. Maybe that's why
it's easy to dismiss. Even when the best prescription for our
heart is prayer, sometimes it feels safer to fight the battles
ourselves or rely on conventional wisdom to figure it out.
Although I've seen prayer work thousands of times in my
life and the lives of others, there are still parts that confuse me. Perhaps that's what makes Miss Clara's resolve so
notable. She knows without a shred of doubt that prayer
is her greatest weapon, and she uses it like a sharpshooter.
This prayer warrior knows that time spent with God is never
wasted.

The truth is that we have to be careful how we think about prayer. We tend to underestimate it. Common thinking tells us that God doesn't hear us when we pray or that He won't always answer us or that we can't ask for what we really want or even that prayer isn't effective. Those are lies. Here's how we know: *"God's there, listening for all who pray, for all who pray and mean it. He does what's best for those who fear him—hears them call out, and saves them"* (Psalm 145:18–19 MSG). When we entertain lies about what prayer is and is not, it's an invitation for the Enemy to enter into our hearts and minds and wreak havoc.

Praying is the last thing he wants us to do. The Enemy knows prayer allows direct access to God. He knows it's the key to pursuing a life of passion and purpose. It brings wisdom, confidence, discernment, peace, comfort, resolve, and whatever else we need in that moment. It helps us process situations with our Father. Prayer gives us freedom to share our hopes and dreams with the One who can make them happen. Instead of communicating with God, the Enemy wants us to live defeated, disillusioned, and discouraged. He wants our worries and concerns to be kept to ourselves.

The Enemy hates you and me and has been plotting against our very existence from the moment we took our first breath. Every day, we're in a war between good and evil. And prayer is our most formidable weapon because it connects us to God's heart immediately and gives us power in all our circumstances. James 5:16 (MSG) proves it: *"The prayer of a person living right with God is something powerful to be reckoned with."*

So why aren't we taking prayer seriously? We are missing out on one of the most significant tools of warfare available to us. Prayer brings the power of heaven down to earth—down to you. And it's an atomic bomb to the Enemy's plans. Rather than harnessing its potency, we're finding reasons not to embrace the power of prayer. Let's look at a few excuses we use.

1) *I Don't Have Time*

No matter how you slice it, life is busy. It's easy to become overwhelmed with to-do lists that seem a mile long. In our family, my husband calls that *task* mode because I become almost militant as I knock things off the list one by one. If anyone or anything gets in my way, chances are there will be casualties.

It's this busyness that can often justify our unwillingness to stop and pray. We think, *Who has time for it with all that must be accomplished?* And so we carry the load ourselves because it feels easier than delegating—even delegating to God. What we forget is that God can order our day to make it manageable. He offers perspective so we can prioritize. And He can fill us with joy as we journey through our to-dos.

2) *God Already Knows*

Have you ever wondered why—if God already knows all that's on our heart—we need to pray? It feels like a waste of time and energy because He already knows our next move before we make it. And while that may be true, what God craves is a relationship with us that's cultivated through time spent together. One way we do that is through prayer.

When my teenagers come home from school, go into their rooms, and close their doors, I miss getting to hear their hearts. I want to know what made their day good or what made it not so good. I want to know how *that* situation worked out. I'm interested in helping them with homework or offering advice. I want to hear every noteworthy event or feeling. Why? Because as their parent, my heart is deeply invested in their lives. The same is true for our heavenly Father. Even if He knows every detail, He wants to hear it from you.

3) *I Don't Have the Right Words*

I'm not sure where we got the idea that our prayers had to be full of the *right* words. Nowhere in the Bible does scripture tell us to change our speaking style when we talk to God. Instead, the Word invites us to come to God as we are with whatever is burdening our heart. We don't have to have the right words—just the right heart. Why? Because we have divine support.

Romans 8:26 (MSG) says, *"If we don't know how or what to pray, it doesn't matter. He does our praying in and for us, making prayer out of our wordless sighs, our aching groans."* The "He" in this verse refers to the Holy Spirit, and His help makes our prayers uncommon. We don't have to change a thing.

I've known women who completely change their speaking style when they pray, sounding terribly formal in prayers. Their words become flowery and lofty, and sometimes I struggle to follow along with what they're saying. Rather than speaking from the heart, they seem more concerned with how their prayer sounds.

When you pray, just talk to God like you talk to someone you love. Don't get caught up in crafting the perfect sentences because you don't need to impress Him. That's a common thought about prayer. Instead, just share from your heart and trust the Holy Spirit to intercede for you.

Having an uncommon prayer life means we talk to God often and about everything because we know it makes all the difference in the world. Hannah knew that all too well. Let's dive into her story from 1 Samuel 1 and 2. You'll soon see why prayer was not only her default button, but also her operating system.

Hannah

Of Elkanah, 1 Samuel 1:2 (TLB) reads, *"He had two wives, Hannah and Peninnah. Peninnah had some children, but Hannah didn't."* And there it is. Maybe you know the pain of infertility. For many women, it's a struggle that drives us to our knees. My husband and I were told we couldn't have kids, and we watched as our friends were having them left and right. Of course God had different plans—we became pregnant with Sam and later Sara a few years into our marriage—but I remember my own season of praying for children. My heart connects with Hannah's.

The ability to have children held great value to the Israelites. It was considered their divine purpose, and because of that, they were recognized as a blessing from God Himself. So a woman unable to have children often battled personal sorrow, a blaming husband, and disapproval from her own family, and was considered *less than* in society. Without children, especially a son, how was the family line to continue? The pressure was on. But rather than hide in shame and fear, Hannah prayed.

I appreciate that God gave Hannah a loving husband in Elkanah. He adored her. But Peninnah, his other wife, was especially cruel and made Hannah's suffering even worse. Rather than respond in kind and dish it right back, Hannah prayed. In her deepest pain and great trials, she went before the Lord in prayer and petition. That is a beautiful picture of uncommon prayer.

At one point, she prayed so passionately that Eli the temple priest thought she was drunk. First Samuel 1:15–16 reads, *"My lord, I am not drunk on wine or any strong drink; I am just a **woman with a wounded spirit**. I have been **pouring out the pain** in my soul before the Eternal One. Please don't consider your servant some worthless woman just because I have been **speaking for so long** out of worry and exasperation"* (VOICE, emphasis mine). Hannah knew God was the only one who could heal her wounded spirit, and so she laid bare her soul. The informality and rawness of her prayers even made Eli question her state. I love Hannah's willingness to be authentic in prayer.

No doubt her plea with God was to be a mom. She desperately wanted a child and pleaded for Him to open her womb. And later in that same chapter, Hannah's prayers are answered and she gives birth to Samuel. God graciously gave her what her heart desired most. She offers us the perfect example of uncommon prayer because she knew it tethered her heart to His.

But I must insert a big truth right here, so buckle up. Ready? *God isn't our magic genie, and we can't manipulate His response to our requests.* Sometimes His answer is *yes*. Other times it's *wait*. And He also answers *no. . .*but He does so only because there's a better *yes* down the road.

Friend, there is no prayer formula to follow that will ensure we get what we want out of God. It doesn't work like that, and we'll be set up for discouragement if we decide the only answer we will accept is a *yes*. Uncommon prayer also means we accept His answers because we trust His plan.

Hannah was a woman of faith, and I'd like to think that means she would have unconditionally accepted the outcome of her request no matter what. She wasn't demanding or angry. Hannah didn't give an ultimatum. But she did share the depth of her hopes and dreams with God, asking for what she wanted. Ultimately, He is all-knowing, and we're most certainly not. If we are going to live uncommon lives as we walk out our faith through prayer, we'll have to choose to accept God's answer.

While we've established there is no recipe for the perfect prayer that yields the perfect outcome, there is a blueprint we can follow.

1) Confess Your Sins

We don't want anything to block the blessing, and unconfessed sin can be an issue. Psalm 66:18 (TLB) reads, *"He would not have listened if I had not confessed my sins."* If we are willfully living in sin and disobedience, it could be a barrier.

2) Ask with the Right Motives

James 4:3 (VOICE) says, *"And when you do ask, you still do not get what you want because your motives are all wrong—because you continually focus on self-indulgence."* Be careful that you aren't asking for all the wrong reasons. If I ask for my book sales to soar, it better be because I want women to live uncommon rather than because I want fame or fortune. Motives matter. And since He knows our heart, it means He also knows what's in it.

3) Use the Precedent Set in Scripture

If God has done it before, He will do it again. I've pleaded with God, asking Him to deliver me from my enemies like He did when the Israelites crossed through the Red Sea. I've asked Him for ministry partners like Aaron was for Moses. I've asked God to remove the scales off of eyes like He did for Paul. It's not that He needs the reminder. It's that we do. It helps us to remember that God is able and willing.

4) Show Gratitude and Respect

Tell God how thankful you are He is in the details, and for all He has already done in your life. I often thank Him for going before me and clearing the path. I tell God how much I love Him and how much I appreciate who He is in my life. Thank Him for being faithful, loving, trustworthy, kind, and capable. . .like Psalm 100:4 (CEB), *"Enter his gates with thanks; enter his courtyards with praise! Thank him! Bless his name!"* This sets your heart right because you're focusing on more than what you need and want. You are focusing on who He is.

5) Ask Away, but Be Prepared to Accept His Answer

We see Paul demonstrate this in 2 Corinthians 12:8–10 (VOICE):

> *I begged the Lord three times to liberate me from its anguish; and finally He said to me, "My grace is enough to cover and sustain you. My power is made perfect in weakness." So ask me about my*

*thorn, inquire about my weaknesses, and I will
gladly go on and on—I would rather stake my
claim in these and have the power of the Anointed
One at home within me. I am at peace and even
take pleasure in any weaknesses, insults, hard-
ships, persecutions, and afflictions for the sake of
the Anointed because when I am at my weakest,
He makes me strong.*

We are invited to ask for anything, but like Paul we trust
when God's answer is different than we had hoped. He
knows exactly what we need, when we need it, and always
has our best in His sights.

Let's choose to be women who thrive because of uncommon prayer. Let's remember that it is a powerful defense
from the Enemy's schemes. We don't have to fall into his
trap—or stay there—anymore. Let's recognize the ways it
strengthens our resolve when the storms of life hit with a
vengeance and never excuse it away again. Let's remember
the five ways we can position ourselves for powerful prayers
that set us up for powerful results. And let's remember to
recognize God for His majesty rather than set our expectation that He is our personal genie in a bottle. When we
know these things and practice them in our prayer life, it
will help us live uncommon for sure.

Lean into Him

*Call to Me, and I will answer you. I will tell
you of great things, things beyond what you can
imagine, things you could never have known.*
(Jeremiah 33:3 VOICE)

Don't fret or worry. Instead of worrying, pray. Let petitions and praises shape your worries into prayers, letting God know your concerns. Before you know it, a sense of God's wholeness, everything coming together for good, will come and settle you down. It's wonderful what happens when Christ displaces worry at the center of your life. (Philippians 4:6–7 MSG)

"The world is full of so-called prayer warriors who are prayer-ignorant. They're full of formulas and programs and advice, peddling techniques for getting what you want from God. Don't fall for that nonsense. This is your Father you are dealing with, and he knows better than you what you need." (Matthew 6:7–18 MSG)

The righteous call to the LORD, and he listens; he rescues them from all their troubles. (Psalm 34:17 GNT)

Look into You

What role does prayer play in your life today? Do you pray more in hard times than good times?

How did your parents or guardians model prayer throughout your childhood?

How do you respond to disappointments or failures in your life? Do they drive you to God or to something or someone else?

Can you remember a time God answered your prayers in an obvious way? How did He provide for you during that time?

How did Hannah's story encourage you or challenge you?

What does uncommon prayer look like to you?

Live Uncommon

Lord, I confess that prayer confuses me and that I sometimes approach Your throne with the wrong motives. I confess I've relied on human efforts too often rather than trust You with parts of my life. Please forgive me. Father, would You remind me to be a prayerful woman in all things? Would You prompt me to connect with You when I forget? I want to be a woman who knows and wields the power of uncommon prayer. Thank You for being accessible to everyone and in all circumstances. There is so much peace and joy in knowing You're willing to meet us anytime we ask. I am so grateful that You are my God! In Jesus' name, amen.

CHAPTER 17

Uncommon Morality

God put the wrong on him who never did anything wrong,
so we could be put right with God.
2 Corinthians 5:21 MSG

*M*orals are the right and wrong of our actions and thoughts. They inform the decisions we make about what should and should not be done—what is good and bad. And over the last several years, it feels like those lines are blurring at record pace. And they are shifting in a direction that greatly opposes God. It's not just you and me who are noticing either. According to a recent Gallup poll, 72 percent of Americans believe our morals are in decline. [12]

We've become a *push-the-envelope* society where it seems nothing is off-limits and everything is embraced and applauded. Sometimes I shake my head and laugh at the stupidity of it all. Other times, I weep in deep sorrow because I don't understand how we got *here*. Regardless, it feels as if we're coming to the end of right and wrong. And all too often, we're compromising what we know is right because we don't want to deal with backlash from speaking out. We're keeping our mouths shut for fear of retribution. Offended people offend people, and many of us have been in the line of fire. Instead of defending our position, we say *no thank you* and stay silent. But now more than ever, it's time to stand in the gap to keep morality in check.

The Bible is very clear about how we are to live—and

how we are not. It offers us a clear vision of what's right and what's wrong. And I've yet to find a topic God does not address in His Word. Sex, money, community, career, parenting, marriage, friendship, mediation, justice, divorce, abuse, infertility, sickness, etc.—it's all in there. The Bible is an all-inclusive blueprint for how to do life with uncommon morality. But are we reading it? Even more, are we following it? It's not about perfection; it's about pursuit. And with the state of our nation and the world, we must pursue it with all we've got. Not just for us, but because what we do now will affect generations to come.

In Galatians 5:19–21 (voice), Paul unpacks what kind of immorality to avoid:

> *It's clear that our flesh entices us into practicing some of its most heinous acts: participating in corrupt sexual relationships, impurity, unbridled lust, idolatry, witchcraft, hatred, arguing, jealousy, anger, selfishness, contentiousness, division, envy of others' good fortune, drunkenness, drunken revelry, and other shameful vices that plague humankind.*

And then he finishes up with a stern warning.

> *I told you this clearly before, and I only tell you again so there is no room for confusion: those who give in to these ways will not inherit the kingdom of God.*

Let's unpack this. Here is the list of choices we can make

that compromise our pursuit of living with uncommon morality because we *know* they are wrong. . .and we do them anyway.

1) corrupt sexual relationships (prostitution, marital affairs, etc.)
2) impurity
3) lust
4) idolatry
5) witchcraft
6) hatred
7) arguing
8) jealousy
9) anger
10) selfishness
11) contentiousness
12) division
13) envy
14) drunkenness
15) and other shameful immoralities that plague us

That is a full list, and when I first read it, I freaked out. I see myself in that list way too many times—and just in the last week. Maybe you do, too. But it's the last sentence of that scripture where I get my hope. It says, *"Those who* **give in** *to* **these ways** *will not inherit the kingdom of God."* Some might see this as scary and ominous, but it affirms my heart and strengthens my bones. So take a deep breath and let me show you why.

If you have asked Jesus to be the Lord of your life, a supernatural exchange took place. In that moment of decision, you chose to exchange *these ways* for *His ways*. And you were given the ability to live with uncommon morality because the Holy Spirit now resides in your heart. While God isn't expecting that you do it perfectly, He is hoping you'll do it purposefully. But rest assured, the salvation you received cannot be taken from you, even if you fall into *these ways* from time to time.

The Holy Spirit is your counselor and convictor of sin (John 16:7–11). And He is the source for uncommon morality. He is the "gut feeling" you get when something doesn't feel right. The Holy Spirit is what sounds the alarm bell when you need to turn from the path you're on. And while our human condition causes us to make bad choices and decisions from time to time, God's Spirit is the one who calls us to live better and gives us the ability to do so.

Life is too short to live tangled up in that list of *these ways*. We can choose to live differently. And if we are going to influence others for God—if we are going to be the salt-seasoning that points out the God-colors in the world—then our lives need to model uncommon morality. Never forget that you have a choice and you have a voice.

Let's not sit by and watch the moral fabric of society continue to fray. We don't have to become rigid and militant, but we're on planet earth on purpose. This isn't dress rehearsal, friend. No, we are living on the stage of life. And if we choose to sit idly by, we are not doing the job we were created to do.

I love the story of Puah and Shiphrah from Exodus 1. These two women didn't sit idle. They didn't give in to sin. No, they were up for the task God put in front of them. They risked their lives to do what was right. They stood up for morality. And God blessed them. Here is their story.

Puah and Shiphrah

Puah and Shiphrah were Hebrew midwives who served as managers over the rest of the Hebrew midwives during a time when the slave population in Egypt was exploding! Pharaoh was noticing the shift in numbers. He was worried that at some point the slaves would outnumber Egyptians and they would stage an uprising. So faced with fear, he decided to take drastic measures. Pharaoh ordered the midwives to kill all Hebrew baby boys at their first breath.

Can you begin to imagine what Puah and Shiphrah were thinking when that decree came down? I imagine their minds were spinning with fear and confusion. I'm sure they were playing out scenarios, trying to make sense of it all. If they had to deliver their best friend's baby, how could they carry out those orders? While they didn't yet have the Ten Commandments, they knew murder was wrong all the way around. Our girls were in an extreme moral dilemma.

But these two had uncommon morality. They feared God more than their own death, which meant there was no way they'd be able to kill newborns or instruct other midwives to follow the decree either. They knew the stakes were high, and they had to navigate this situation carefully and prayerfully. That powerful combination brought divine revelation, and because of it every newborn Hebrew boy lived.

Scripture tells us that when Pharaoh discovered this, he sent for the midwives and asked why they had disobeyed. They responded, *"Because unlike Egyptian women, Hebrew women are hearty and energetic, and they give birth before the midwife arrives to help"* (Exodus 1:19 VOICE). But in truth, they decided to procrastinate their arrival until after the women had given birth. And under these two midwives, the Hebrew population continued to expand. The nation of Israel became stronger and more powerful.

And you know what else, verse 21 (VOICE) says, *"Because the midwives respected God, He blessed them with families of their own."* I love this. It's incentive. When we choose to respect and obey God's ways and will, there's a blessing that comes with it. And living with uncommon morality pleases God more than following the ever-changing group-think of our world. We may not live in a moral society, but we can create an uncommon moral home. We can raise children who respect the Word of God. We can live in ways that please Him as best as we can.

Anna

Anna was a prophetess who lived in a time when being a woman did *not* have its privileges. She had a short marriage of seven years and chose to live her eighty-four widow years fasting and praying in the temple. Luke 2:37 says she *never left*, and she *worshiped day and night*. But because she was a woman, she was denied access to the temple proper. Instead, Anna had to stay in the outer court established for women.

I might have thought, *Okay, I've put in the time here, and at some point they need to invite me into the temple.* I might have felt a little left out. I might have been bitter or frustrated. I may have wondered if people were talking behind my back, commenting on how I needed to get on with my life. But not Anna. There is no indication in scripture that she ever felt anything but love and gratitude toward God and others.

She didn't get weighted down by what others might be thinking or what society considered acceptable. She didn't compromise her heart. She didn't wallow in self-pity. She didn't let it interfere with her love and adoration of God. The times may have restricted her from entering the temple with the men, but that never restricted how she felt about God. Anna knew the difference between right and wrong, and she chose to live upright and grateful. That is uncommon morality, and God blessed her for it.

Luke 2:38 (TLB) tells us, *"She came along just as Simeon was talking with Mary and Joseph, and she also began thanking God and telling everyone in Jerusalem who had been awaiting the coming of the Savior that the Messiah had finally arrived."* What perfect timing. God allowed Anna to be one of the first to bear witness to Jesus. He orchestrated such a sweet gift to a woman who had dedicated her life to living right and loving the Lord.

I hope you caught the end result from both stories. For Puah, Shiphrah, and Anna, God blessed their pursuit of uncommon morality. And because there has been a precedent set in scripture, it means we can also receive the blessing that comes from pursuing an upright life. Believe me, I know living that way isn't easy. Or popular. Our pride, our desire to fit in, our weak-mindedness, and our insecurities make it hard to live with conviction. And trying to walk out uncommon morality sets us up for ridicule and judgment. We risk being labeled as narrow-minded or intolerant. But for Pete's sake, let's find our divine backbone.

So how do we live an uncommon moral life? Sometimes we forget about the moral code of conduct God has already given us in scripture. It's called the Ten Commandments, and they are our set of directives. The first five relate to living morally *with God*, and the last five are ways to live morally *with others*. Let's unpack them together.

1) Do Not Worship Any Other God Other Than the One True God.

There were eight major false gods named in the Old Testament. Today, though, there are countless gods and deities worshipped through countless different religions: Hinduism, Islam, Buddhism, New Age, to name a few. In these religions, relationships with the gods are based on rituals and performance. In Christianity, the focus is on a personal relationship with God through Jesus Christ. It's law versus grace. The choice seems so clear.

2) Do Not Make Idols or Images in the Form of God.

Whatever gets your time and attention can often become an idol. It can be someone or something, and we can begin to worship it with our affection. It could be a husband or a child. It could be money, exercise, television, work, alcohol, or anything we decide is more important than our relationship with Him. He is a jealous God, and He wants you to put Him above all else.

3) Do Not Use God's Name with Disrespect.

When we speak the name of God, it should always be with reverence and regard. He is the Creator of the universe and everything in it, and because of that His name should be used with the highest esteem. There is nothing uglier and more offensive than hearing someone take His name in vain. That includes saying "Oh my God" when used as an expletive or in excitement. Let's always speak His name with morality.

4) Set Aside One Day Each Week for Rest.

God is reminding us to give our minds, souls, and spirits a break from the hustle and bustle of life. He knows how hard we work. He knows how busy our to-do lists keep us. This is divinely inspired self-care, and it's an opportunity to refuel your body, regroup your thoughts, and reconnect with God.

5) Treat Your Mother and Father with Respect.

Sometimes this is a tall order, especially when we've been raised in an abusive home. But God is not asking you to place yourself in danger or be a doormat for more abuse. Instead, He is asking you recognize them as authority figures, speaking kindly to and of them, because God chose them specifically for you.

6) Do Not Murder.

This not only means the deliberate act of killing someone but also hating them in your heart. When we wish hurt or heartache on another, it counts. Our words and actions can be the sword that kills the dreams or esteem of another. We may not like everyone, but we are called to respect them.

7) Keep Sex within the Boundaries of Marriage.

God put this in place so we would learn to respect our bodies. This also ensures we receive the blessing that comes from purity until marriage. Every time we give ourselves to someone other than our spouse, a soul tie is created. And that keeps us connected to that person in a supernatural way, bringing them and our intimate exchange into our marriage. This is a hard command to keep, but one that provides much fruit!

8) Do Not Steal.

God is asking us to respect people and their property. The command is straightforward. If what you want isn't yours, then you do not have the freedom to take it. It's yours when someone gives it to you or when you purchase it. If none of those apply, then leave it.

9) Do Not Lie.

When we gossip and spread rumors about someone, more times than not it is laced with lies. When we stretch or withhold the truth or when we give a different version of the truth, we are lying, too. God is asking us to be truth tellers in all we do.

10) Do Not Covet.

This is a call for us to be content. When we compare ourselves to others. . .when we crave their lives or marriages or stuff. . .when we give into jealousy and envy—we are being ungrateful for what God has given us. Instead of looking at them, focus on the blessing God has given to you. This is a recipe for the divine perspective we need to be content.

And there you have it. Ten ways we can live our one and only life with uncommon morality. It may not be easy, but it will be worth it. Contrast this against the world's warped idea of morality today and you'll see why we need to live differently. God is asking us to be the moral barometer in a nation that seems to be turning its back on Him and *His ways*. We have the privilege to influence our corner of the world. And here's what we're up against.

- A society that tells us to do whatever feels good.
- A culture that tells us not to care about consequences because there are no longer moral absolutes.
- An agenda that discourages us from taking a stand for what's right because it could offend others.
- A movement that encourages us to let go of moral boundaries because they're old and out of date.

And even more, if we don't embrace the world's perversion and unbridled freedom, we're criticized for being too holy, too judgmental, and too narrow-minded. Friend, every day is a combat zone for uncommon morality—the kind of living that pleases God. It's time to put on our big-girl pants and stand confident in what we know is right. Because when we do, our actions and words will be like salt-seasoning, flavoring the world with God's name. And we will be blessed.

Lean into Him

So roll up your sleeves, put your mind in gear, be totally ready to receive the gift that's coming when Jesus arrives. Don't lazily slip back into those old grooves of evil, doing just what you feel like doing. You didn't know any better then; you do now. As obedient children, let yourselves be pulled into a way of life shaped by God's life, a life energetic and blazing with holiness. God said, "I am holy; you be holy." (1 Peter 1:13–16 MSG)

"The Helper, the Holy Spirit, whom the Father will send in my name, will teach you everything and make you remember all that I have told you." (John 14:26 GNT)

But don't be so naïve—there's another saying you know well—Bad company corrupts good habits. (1 Corinthians 15:33 VOICE)

You must be doers of the word and not only hearers who mislead themselves. Those who hear but don't do the word are like those who look at their faces in a mirror. They look at themselves, walk away, and immediately forget what they were like. But there are those who study the perfect law, the law of freedom, and continue to do it. They don't listen and then forget, but they put it into practice in their lives. They will be blessed in whatever they do. (James 1:22–25 CEB)

Blessed are those who work for justice, who always do what they know to be right! (Psalm 106:3 VOICE)

Look into You

What would you say is the biggest moral failure in the world today? How might it offend God?

As we looked at Galatians 5:19–21, what were your thoughts? Was it discouraging? Encouraging? Challenging? Why?

In what ways do you protect morality in your life and your home? Or in what ways will you begin to live differently so you become an agent of change?

We looked at the ways Puah, Shiphrah, and Anna lived with uncommon morality. What connected to your heart the most about their stories?

The Ten Commandments are our moral code of ethics. They're just as relevant today as when Moses carried them down the mountain. What did the Holy Spirit show you through them?

How will you live with uncommon morality?

Live Uncommon

Lord, sometimes I am so overwhelmed by the state of the world. I see lines being crossed and barriers broken that usher in evil and perversion. It often leaves me feeling helpless. Hopeless. And I wonder what I can do. I feel small compared to the issues of immorality that are changing the fabric of my country. I've also messed up so many times and made choices that I know offended You. Please forgive me. I want to live differently. So, Father, would You give me a boldness to stand for what is right? I need Your courage so I can stand strong in my own life. I want to point others to You. I want to be a world changer, Lord. Please use me to stand in the gap for morality. I love You. In Jesus' name, amen.

CHAPTER 18

Uncommon Wisdom

*Trust GOD from the bottom of your heart; don't try to
figure out everything on your own. Listen for GOD's voice
in everything you do, everywhere you go; he's the one who
will keep you on track. Don't assume that you know it all.*
Proverbs 3:5–6 MSG

Walking down the aisle, I knew it was wrong. I was
making a huge mistake. But the dress was paid for, the
flowers were arranged, the guests had flown in, the cake was
decorated, and my wounded heart couldn't bear to admit
what it already knew—this was not the man I was supposed
to marry.

Just a few days earlier, we talked about our concerns.
We both saw the huge warning flags waving furiously in the
wind but felt continuing on with the wedding was the best
decision. We chalked it up to prewedding jitters. However, it
was so much more than that. It was the Holy Spirit letting
us know this was not God's will. I was just too broken and
desperate for love to heed the warning.

Rather than listen, I decided pure grit could pull us
through and we could learn to love one another. I thought
with enough gumption, our marriage would work. Even
though our premarital counselor said he didn't believe we
were compatible, I ignored it. My baby sister had married
earlier that year, and I felt the pressure to keep up. So I put
on a confident smile and went through the motions. And on

our two-year anniversary, my marriage was officially over.

I was full of wrong motives and misguided optimism, and it didn't take long to realize you can't build a marriage on them. Counseling couldn't fix us, our gumption ran out, and we walked away even more broken. Had I listened to God's warning, I could have avoided the heartache. Sometimes we ignore the Holy Spirit's guidance. Other times we forget that divine wisdom is accessible if we ask. Instead, we do what we want.

There are many reasons we make bad choices.

- We justify that because everyone else is doing it, we should, too.
- We poll our friends and family for their thoughts and then decide our next step based on the consensus.
- We make wrong choices because we don't think we deserve any better.
- We let fear guide us.
- We need to make a quick decision and don't get all the facts first.
- We decide we don't need God's input.
- We manipulate the situation to confirm our narrative.

But when we lean on our worldly wisdom alone instead of aligning it with God's wisdom, we get into trouble. Our insight can be spot-on at times, but His is complete and absolute. And even more, it's available to us. We don't have to wander through life *hoping* we're making the right decisions. Instead, we can be certain if we're choosing wisely or not. We have a powerful tool for accessing uncommon wisdom.

*"**All of Scripture** is God-breathed; in its inspired voice, we*

hear useful teaching, rebuke, correction, instruction, and training
for a life that is right so that God's people may be up to the task
ahead and **have all they need** *to* **accomplish every** *good work*"
(2 Timothy 3:16–17 VOICE, emphasis mine).

Gosh, I love the Word of God. It's chock-full of truths
that help us walk out uncommon lives. And this scripture
from 2 Timothy reminds us that God doesn't leave us to figure life out on our own—praise the Lord! Instead, He gives
us exactly what we need to do life well. Let's break that verse
down so you'll see what I mean.

Every Word Is from God

Critics want us to believe the Bible is written from a
human perspective and is full of made-up stories and author
opinions and is no longer relevant to life today. That could
not be further from the truth. Of course God used people
to pen the Bible, but He has told us that every word written
was *inspired* by Him. And since we choose to believe the
scriptures in their entirety, we can trust that every word,
verse, and book came from Him.

Every Word Teaches Us

The Bible is life's blueprint for His followers. So when
we spend time digging in it, exploring it, and meditating on
it, we naturally learn from it. Here's how:

1) It reveals our mistakes.
2) It course corrects our path.
3) It affirms our decisions.
4) It firms up our understanding of right and wrong.

And you know what? There has never been a moment when I've been disappointed after spending time in the Word. Every single time I sit in its pages, I benefit. So will you.

Every Word Equips Us

When the scripture says it equips us to "*accomplish every good work,*" I believe it means we'll be able to know the difference between good and bad. Time in the Word will give us uncommon wisdom to make the right choices. It will offer us divine insight and knowledge. But we still have to choose which path we'll take. And the question becomes, will we be wise based on the Word or on the world?

Let's look at two women from the Bible who offer us compelling examples of uncommon wisdom.

Abigail

Abigail is known for being one the Bible's greatest peacemakers and was married to a wealthy rancher named Nabal. Scripture says she was smart and beautiful, but her husband was bad-tempered and mean-spirited. And where she was full of wisdom, he was not. Opposites do attract, right? You can find their story in 1 Samuel 25.

We watch the scene open with David and company camped near the couple's land. These were the pre-king years when he was more of an outlaw than royalty. And because it was sheep-shearing season, David's men helped Nabal's shepherds with their work. Rather than attack Nabal's employees and take the sheep for themselves, they helped protect instead. So when David sent his men to ask Nabal to be paid for their work—work the shepherds confirmed as true and valuable—the request was denied. Instead, he insulted David, and it did not go over well.

In his anger, David set out to destroy Nabal's household. First Samuel 25:13 (VOICE) says, *"Strap on your swords! All of them put on their swords, including David, and about 400 of his men followed him while 200 remained behind with their supplies."* Luckily, one of Nabal's servants heard the exchange and gave Abigail the heads-up.

She knew the stakes were high, so she immediately loaded up donkeys with two hundred loaves of bread, two jugs of wine, five sheep ready for cooking, more than fifty quarts of roasted grain, two hundred clusters of raisins, and two hundred fig cakes. And then she told her servants, *"Go ahead of me with all the gifts. I'll be right behind you"* (v. 19 VOICE). She was going to intercept David without her husband's knowledge, initiate a potentially dangerous meeting, and try to keep the peace. She had a plan.

When she saw David, she fell to the ground in front of him, bowing. God inspired in her the right words and actions that would stop David's plans for destruction. She started by reminding him of his character and values. She reminded him that he was one who fought on behalf of God and that *"no evil will be found in you as long as you live"* (v. 28 VOICE). She suggested that if he killed her husband, it would anger one of the tribes of Israel he would soon rule over, potentially causing big issues down the road. And because of her uncommon wisdom, David's eyes were opened. He had a change of heart.

In that moment, David recognized that God sent her to bring perspective. *"Blessed is the Eternal God of Israel, who sent you here today to intercept me. And blessed is your wisdom— blessed are you—for keeping me from shedding blood needlessly* and from taking vengeance into my own hands" (vv. 32–33, VOICE). So he accepted her gifts, granted her wish, and sent her home. No one in the house of Nabal was killed that day at the hands of David and his men.

When she told Nabal about the exchange the next morning, scripture said he went cold inside. And ten days later, he died. But here's my favorite part. Verse 40 (VOICE) reads, *"Then David sent servants to Carmel asking Abigail to be his wife."* She said yes, mounted her donkey once again, and went directly to David.

Is that a great love story or what? Abigail won him over with her diplomacy. She didn't play dumb. She didn't keep her mouth shut when she knew a better way. And she didn't sit around and wait for her husband to come around. God's discernment stirred in her heart and gave her the confidence she needed to take a bold step of faith forward. She demonstrated uncommon wisdom and the payoff was huge.

The Wise Woman of Abel Beth-Maacah

Second Samuel 20:15 sets the foundation for our story. It reads, *"Then Joab's men arrived and attacked Sheba at Abel of Beth-maacah. They piled up a ramp against the city, and it stood against the outer wall. All of Joab's troops were hammering the wall, trying to bring it down"* (CEB).

Joab was following King David's orders to hunt down Sheba because he had turned David's men against him. All men except those from Judah deserted David at Sheba's prompting, and he was furious. When they arrived at Abel, Joab's men were prepared to knock down the city wall to kill Sheba, who was hiding inside.

But there was a woman who had the wisdom she needed

to act quickly and save her city. Scripture tells us she cried out, asking to meet with Joab. What boldness. What clarity in purpose! Can you just picture the scene? Through the pounding and screaming of the army beating on the wall. . . with the city's inhabitants full of fear. . .this unnamed woman had the courage to ask for the guy in charge.

And because she knows much is at stake, she says, *"Pay close attention to the words of your female servant"* (v. 17 CEB). She reminds him of Abel's reputation as one of Israel's mother cities, full of peaceful and reliable people. She then asks why he would want to mess with God that way. But Joab quickly cleared up the confusion, letting her know they weren't there to harm the city; they were there to find a man.

In her wisdom, she made a deal. Joab promised to stop the destruction and she promised that *"his head will be thrown over the wall to you"* (v. 21 CEB). And both kept good on their word. She knew there was no room for error. And she measured her words with sound judgment because of it.

We can learn from her uncommon wisdom. It gave her the insight to step into a messy situation. It gave her the right words that would appeal to Joab's compassion. It gave her a no-nonsense game plan. And in the end, her judiciousness gave everyone what they wanted in the first place.

Do you know what I'd imagine these two women had in common? They must have known God and His heart so well—through prayer and the prophet's teachings—that His wisdom already flowed through their veins. They made quick and confident decisions because of it. And when God's game plan stirred in their hearts, they obeyed. What an asset to their families and communities.

But sometimes we struggle to know if the game plan is from Him or if our own agenda is getting in the way. Let's look at some ways God speaks to us.

Through Consistent and Persistent Messages

When I'm waiting on the Lord for answers and direction, sometimes I begin to see a pattern of messages in my life. There was a season a few years back where the phrase *Life is Good* was everywhere I turned. Bumper stickers, tote bags, T-shirts, online graphics, etc. It was so profuse that I started laughing every time I came across it. It was as if God was speaking directly to me—like He wanted me to know life really was good. And every time a life storm hits, my mind goes back to that divine reminder almost every time.

Through Scripture

Sometimes scripture jumps right off the page and connects with my heart in a profound way. I feel like God is telling me that certain words are just for me and my situation. The Bible is alive and active and full of wisdom even for today's problems. So when I write the date next to a passage that God directs me to, it's a visual reminder that He meets me in the pages of His Word. Honestly, I cannot think of a time when I closed the Bible in frustration.

Through a Sermon

Have you ever felt like the pastor is talking directly to you? Or have you ever felt the heat of the proverbial spotlight shining on your head—certain everyone is watching you squirm in your seat? Oh yes, been there, done that. So often, my time in the pew is when God downloads insight into something I am struggling to manage.

Through a Song

I don't know about you, but music moves me to tears more times than not. I grew up making fun of my mom for always crying through worship time at church, and now my kids make fun of me. And while I love today's worship songs that take me right to the throne room, there are old hymns that reduce me to a blubbering idiot. Their words move deep in my heart, and I am reminded of His sovereignty. Sometimes that is all the wisdom I need right there.

Through Prayer

When I really dig into prayer rather than simply go through my laundry list of needs, I feel God as close as my next breath. It brings comfort and peace and often a sense of what to do next in my circumstance. Prayer brings us close to the heart of our Father, which helps us see life from His perspective.

Through Other People

Sometimes I hear God loud and clear through the words of someone else. Usually it's a confirmation of what God has already been speaking to me. Their words just bring it to full bloom. While we have wise friends who love Jesus, be careful not to let them become a substitute for His wisdom in your life. Always confirm their advice with Him. He will let you know if it's the way He wants you to go.

If we want to be women who live with uncommon wisdom, then we have to remember God is the source of it. James 1:5 (VOICE) tells us, *"If you don't have all the wisdom* needed for this journey, then all you have to do is ask God for it; and God will grant all that you need. He gives lavishly and never scolds you for asking." So. . .ask. Because He has an endless supply to give you, and your request for it never grows old.

And never forget, it's His wisdom through us that births our ability to live uncommon.

Lean into Him

The man who knows right from wrong and has good judgment and common sense is happier than the man who is immensely rich! For such wisdom is far more valuable than precious jewels. Nothing else compares with it. Wisdom gives: a long, good life, riches, honor, pleasure, peace. Wisdom is a tree of life to those who eat her fruit; happy is the man who keeps on eating it. (Proverbs 3:13–18 TLB)

But you tell me, "With age comes wisdom, and a long life grants understanding." With God is the sum total of all wisdom and of all power; His is the greatest of plans and the deepest of comprehensions. (Job 12:12–13 VOICE)

See to it, then, that no one enslaves you by means of the worthless deceit of human wisdom, which comes from the teachings handed down by human beings and from the ruling spirits of the universe, and not from Christ. (Colossians 2:8 GNT)

Stupid people always think they are right. Wise people listen to advice. (Proverbs 12:15 GNT)

Become wise by walking with the wise; hang out with fools and watch your life fall to pieces. (Proverbs 13:20 MSG)

Look into You

How was wisdom modeled in your home growing up? Did you watch your parents seek God, or did they seek worldly wisdom? What were the results?

Can you think of a time when your wisdom failed you? Thinking back, can you remember warning signs and alarm bells? How would you have handled things differently knowing what you know now?

What were your thoughts on Abigail and the wise woman from Abel? What from their story connected to your heart the most?

We looked at some ways that God speaks uncommon wisdom into our lives. Which ones could you relate to the most? What did you learn through that section?

How would your life be different if you asked God for wisdom rather than solely relying on ideas and suggestions from others?

Live Uncommon

Lord, forgive me for being wise in my own eyes at times. I know discernment and knowledge come from You, and I want to be filled with uncommon wisdom so I can make choices that glorify You! Help me be an Abigail in today's world, ready to act in ways that promote peace and understanding. Just as I am desperate for godly perspective, so is our society. We need Your prudence to replace our foolishness now more than ever. I pray that You would fill me with wise words and actions that influence those around me to pursue the same in their own lives. Also, help me know Your voice when I am faced with hard choices and tricky circumstances. I want to make the right decisions! I love You, Lord! In Jesus' name, amen.

CHAPTER 19

Why the World Needs You to Be Uncommon

As I write this last chapter, Donald Trump was just elected the forty-fifth president of the United States. This was—hands down—the nastiest campaign season I've ever lived through. I cannot believe the venom each candidate spewed at the other. The ads were vicious, heartless, and filled with lies and half-truths. The "dirt" made public was almost unbelievable. And it has been challenging to navigate the last year and a half through unprecedented tactics to polarize a nation. But believe it or not, that isn't what bothered me the most.

Well-known Christian leaders joined in the conversation. Of course they have the right—*and often the call*—to share what they feel God has put on their heart. But this was different. Instead, many implored us to vote a certain way and told us supporting the other candidate was misguided and would reveal our faithlessness. They were reckless with their words. It seems Christian celebrity has gotten out of balance, and I saw it so clearly during this season. I am about to take a little detour but will circle back around in a bit. Ready?

Somewhere along the way, we decided these "celebrities" were more holy than us. We decided their way of thinking was more accurate. We consider them the truth and the way, sometimes more than we do Jesus because we get the Word through them rather than digging into the Bible ourselves. And while it may not have been their intent, many of us have placed them in the category of untouchable. We've elevated them, and it's radically affecting our willingness to live uncommon. We think, *Why even try?*

Since we consider them exceptional and often flawless, we see *them* as uncommon. And since we are not *them*, we decide that uncommon living isn't available to women like *us*. Any effort is futile. We obsess over these women, envious of what we believe is their perfect marriage, perfect family, perfect fashion, perfect words, and perfect godly insight. . . and it becomes an anchor to drown us. Our obsession becomes an excuse to settle for ordinary. We think *if only* I had what they had or could do what they do. . .*then* uncommon would be attainable. But friend, nothing could be further from the truth.

This is where I offer perspective. This is your wake-up call. These women may be called to preach the Good News to a larger audience, but they are not better than you. God gave you a mind of your own that can discern right and wrong just as much as theirs. Perfection is a lie and not the goal of uncommon living. If nothing else, please hear that truth loud and clear.

You have the same level of access to God as someone who stands on platforms or writes books. He doesn't love them any more or any less than He does you. You were given a brain and a heart and God's Spirit as a guide for a reason. And because of that, you have everything you need to live with a powerful purpose. Okay, I'm off my soapbox now and circling back to our conversation. Are you still with me?

Now remember, it wasn't the nasty presidential campaign

tactics or the unsolicited advice from Christian celebrities that bothered me the most about the 2016 election season. But here is what did.

The most disturbing part of it all was watching my Christian friends—just everyday people like you and me—abandon uncommon living and roll in the mud like so many others. Friends and family were pitted against one another. They lashed out in hateful and hurtful ways on social media, tearing each other apart for leaning toward one party or the other. On Facebook, one friend's niece updated her status by asking that family members who voted for the *other* candidate unfriend her because she wanted nothing to do with them anymore. It's true. I can't make stuff like this up.

Rather than listen, everyone was screaming why *their* candidate was the best and why the other one wasn't. And for the past eighteen months or so, the nation's unrest has been loud. It's been hard to see any difference between Jesus lovers and Jesus haters. Even now, several weeks after the election, we are still screaming at one another. Bill Johnson, pastor of Bethel Church in California, saw it, too. He was quoted saying, "In my 40 plus years of ministry, I have never seen those who confess to be followers of Jesus Christ curse and accuse at that level."[13] What are we doing?

I'll be honest, though, at times I wanted to unleash my wrath on someone for their narrow-minded opinion. I wanted to tell a certain few to shut their piehole. I felt the pull to weigh in on a conversation, sharing my frustration. But I chose not to. Why? Because my motives weren't pure and my heart wasn't right, and it would have done nothing but get me into trouble (like it has a million times before). So instead, I kept my mouth shut publicly and shared my exasperation with my husband, a few trusted friends, and God.

And you know what I realized through it all? Uncommon living doesn't mean we won't struggle. It doesn't mean we'll never be tempted to misuse our words and actions. It doesn't mean we won't royally mess up, hurting someone we love. Nor does it mean we will always make the best choices or that our lives will always point others to God. Remember, living uncommon isn't about perfect living. It's about purposeful living.

But—and it's a big *but*—uncommon living does mean we realize our words and actions can either (1) reveal God or (2) be used as weapons to hurt others, incite anger, divide community, or destroy our ability to witness to someone who needs Jesus. And it all comes down to one thing—choice. Who will you choose to be? How will you choose to live?

Those are good questions, ones we all have to answer for ourselves. Choice is one of the greatest gifts God has given to us. In every situation, in every circumstance, in every relationship, and every day, we get to decide how we're going to impact our corner of the world.

The call on your life—the call on my life—is to be a beacon of light and hope for the lost. God has invited us to be a part of something bigger and has baked into every believer's heart the desire and ability to live uncommon. And when we choose that way of living, it opens the eyes of others to see Him. How wonderful is that?

God is inviting us to partner in His plan by becoming uncommon women. And it is verses like Matthew 5:13–16 that confirm we have an awesome purpose and destiny.

"Let me tell you why you are here. You're here to be salt-seasoning that brings out the God-flavors of this earth. If you lose your saltiness, how will people taste godliness? You've lost your usefulness and will end up in the garbage. Here's another way to put it: You're here to be light, bringing out the God-colors in the world. God is not a secret to be kept. We're going public with this, as public as a city on a hill. If I make you light-bearers, you don't think I'm going to hide you under a bucket, do you? I'm putting you on a light stand. Now that I've put you there on a hilltop, on a light stand—shine! Keep open house; be generous with your lives. By opening up to others, you'll prompt people to open up with God, this generous Father in heaven." (MSG)*

We unpacked this scripture in detail in chapter 2, but I felt it fitting to close with this verse as well. Let's never forget we have purpose, and how we live our one and only life on planet earth matters. This passage is a powerful reminder that we each have a corner of the world to influence. And if we are purposeful with our words and actions, we will add flavor and light everywhere we go, and God in heaven will be glorified. Sounds easy, right?

Well, here is where it gets really tricky. This is how we get discouraged, give up, and fall back into our common, ordinary ways. Sometimes our efforts to live uncommon offend others—maybe even our friends and family. Our choices will rub someone the wrong way. We might feel led to take a stand or speak truth drenched in love, but it may insult or upset someone we care about. Deep down, don't we all want to be liked?

The last thing we want to do is make waves because sometimes we end up with a tsunami of backlash we didn't see coming. We may be called prudish or judgmental or holier-than-thou. They might think we're getting too big for our britches, especially because they know the evil ways of our past—something they don't want us to forget. We might even be labeled as hypocrites or frauds because we mess up from time to time. People can be so intolerant of change.

Look, I know there are a million reasons *not* to choose the uncommon way. Some are based in fear. Others are based in pride. You may feel too insecure to risk standing out in a crowd. I know it may rock the boat and change the way you live. Yes, there could be opposition from societal pressures to how your family has always operated to your own habits and hang-ups.

It may take all you have to muster confidence to speak up or follow wisdom to shut up. Everything in you may want to put someone in their place rather than show grace. You may want to be right more than you want to be kind. Change takes courage. And the hard truth is that uncommon ways can also be unpopular ways.

So what do we do when living uncommon lives feels too hard and overwhelming? What if we keep messing up and feel unworthy of the call? How do we swim upstream in waters polluted in every evil way? How can we add flavor and light to a world that glorifies all the wrong things? What do we do when we're scared of being rejected or humiliated or ineffective?

We choose to live uncommon. . .anyway.

If there is anything we've learned from the pages of this book—digging into scripture and learning about women who've gone before us—God will bless us for pursuing purpose and passion as we try to live differently. Friend, your resolve will not go unnoticed in the eyes of God. And with the Holy Spirit as your guide, you can do hard things. Yes, even you.

As an uncommon woman, you will find yourself

> . . .relying on God above all else,
> . . .full of hope in the hard places,
> . . .standing up for what's right,
> . . .holding on to joy no matter what,
> . . .able to step out of your comfort zone,
> . . .willing to risk your reputation,
> . . .resolved not to give up or give in,
> . . .untangled from your past failures, fears,
>   and insecurities,
> . . .capable of looking past your circumstances,
> . . .understanding there is a calling on your life,
> . . .and trusting the plan and ways of God.

Those make a powerful combination, my friend. This is what uncommon living is all about. And remember that Matthew 5:16 reminds us that when we live differently—when we flavor and light the world—others will celebrate God. He will become known to them. *"Keep open house; be generous with your lives. By opening up to others, you'll prompt people to open up with God, this generous Father in heaven"* (msg). And friend, your uncommon life will be why.

You have the opportunity to be a life changer. This is

your official invitation to join in the uncommon movement. The world needs women like you—women willing to stand up for what is good and true and right—to model what a remarkable life in Christ looks like. Not because you are perfect, but because you are purposeful to live rare.

We need to see your resolve to live uncommon, even when it's unpopular. Even when it's hard. Because the next generation needs an example of what intentional living looks like. Being salt and light isn't only a calling; it's the greatest privilege and responsibility we will ever have. And unless we model it in our own lives, others won't know what uncommon living looks like.

So no matter the mistakes you've made, the bridges you've burned, the moral failures you've committed, the painful words you've spewed, the hurtful things you have done—no matter your fears and insecurities, no matter your long list of excuses—with Jesus, you have all you need to be uncommon.

And friend, the world needs you now.

Endnotes

1. "Mordecai Refuses to Bow Down to Haman," Bible Hub, http://biblehub.com/sermons/auth/taylor /mordecai_refuses_to_bow_down_to_haman.htm.

2. "End-Times Persecution Is Here: Russia Just Banned Evangelism and China Has Torn Down Thousands of Crosses," Charisma News, http://www.charismanews. com/opinion/58545-end-times-persecution-is-here- russia-just-banned-evangelism-and-china-has-torn- down-thousands-of-crosses.

3. "Charles Spurgeon," AZ Quotes, http://www.azquotes. com/quote/1411293.

4. Robert Brault quotes, Goodreads, https://www.goodreads. com/author/quotes/7192677.Robert_Brault.

5. Max Lucado quotes, Goodreads, http://www.goodreads. com/quotes/45952-forgiveness-is-unlocking-the-door- to-set-someone-free-and.

6. Frank A. Clark quotes, Thinkexist, http://thinkexist. com/quotation/real-generosity-is-doing-something- nice-for/406611.html.

7. "Mother Teresa of Calcutta—Quotes and Stories," Cross- roads Initiative, https://www.crossroadsinitiative.com/ saints/quotes-from-blessed-mother-teresa-of-calcutta/.

8. *Matthew Henry's Commentary*, BibleGateway, https://www.biblegateway.com/resources/matthew- henry/Gal.5.13-Gal.5.26.

9. Scot McKnight, *The Blue Parakeet: Rethinking How You Read the Bible* (Grand Rapids, MI: Zondervan, 2008), via Google Books, https://books.google.com/books?id=Tqe7CwAAQBAJ&pg=PT104&lpg=PT104&dq=%E2%80%9CHuldah+is+not+chosen+because+no+men+were+available.++She+is+chosen+because+she+is+truly+exceptional+among+the+prophets.%E2%80%9D&source=bl&ots=usMz0Vis2&sig=bF_5koepPO0O1zvV8P74CibRuhA&hl=en&sa=X&ved=0ahUKEwjCoaWy8trOAhWK5yYKHcZaBHsQ6AEIHjAA#v=onepage&q=%E2%80%9CHuldah%20is%20not%20chosen%20because%20no%20men%20were%20available.%20%20She%20is%20chosen%20because%20she%20is%20truly%20exceptional%20among%20the%20prophets.%E2%80%9D&f=false.

10. "The Rabbis' View on Huldah the Prophetess," *Dr. Claude Mariottini—Professor of Old Testament blog*, https://claudemariottini.com/2013/09/24/the-rabbis-view-on-huldah-the-prophetess/.

11. C. S. Lewis quotes, Goodreads, https://www.goodreads.com/quotes/23356-love-is-not-affectionate-feeling-but-a-steady-wish-for

12. "Majority in U.S. Still Say Moral Values Getting Worse," Gallup, https://www.gallup.com/poll/183467/majority-say-moral-values-getting-worse.aspx

13. "Bill Johnson Shares His Pain after Massive Attacks for Defending His Trump Vote," Charisma News, https://www.charismanews.com/opinion/watchman-on-the-wall/61243-bill-johnson-shares-his-pain-after-massive-attacks-for-defending-his-trump-vote

About the Author

Carey Scott is an author, speaker, and certified biblical life coach who loves to have honest conversations about real life. She discusses the issues women struggle with the most, always reminding that perfection is not the goal. Through her ministry, she sets the challenge to stop living a mediocre, risk-free life and instead step onto the battlefield of life and engage! Carey lives in Northern Colorado with her family. Learn more at CareyScott.org.

If You Liked This Book, You'll Also Like...

Choosing Real
by Bekah Jane Pogue

In *Choosing REAL*, author Bekah Pogue walks with women into life's unplanned circumstances—specifically frantic schedules, pain and transition, feelings of unworthiness, loneliness, and tension. . . And she reminds them it is in these very moments that God invites us to notice, respond, and even celebrate how He shows up—in every little detail.
Paperback / 978-1-63409-964-6 / $14.99

When God Says "Wait"
by Elizabeth Laing Thompson

Author Elizabeth Laing Thompson invites readers to walk alongside people of the Bible who had to wait on God. . . like David, Joseph, Miriam, and Naomi. Their stories will equip us to live our own stories—particularly our problematic waiting times—with faith, patience, perspective, and a healthy dose of humor.
Paperback / 978-1-68322-012-1 / $14.99